Azzurra D'Agostino

DREAMS & SYMBOLS

300 SIMPLE WAYS TO DECODE YOUR DREAMS

Illustrations by Federica De Fazio

Vivida

CONTENTS

* BODY

✳ ANIMALS

✳ ACTIONS AND HUMAN RELATIONS

✳ ELEMENTS AND SYMBOLIC FIGURES

* PLACES

DREAMS & SYMBOLS

Every night, our minds, reviewing our daytime experiences and enriching them with elements of the unconscious, pull us each into the mysterious, elusive spaces of dreams. Each person's gender, clothes, or personal symbolic, fantastical universe notwithstanding, there are elements that remain constant, repeating themselves from dream to dream, person to person. Not only do these bring unity to our night journeys, but they serve as universal coordinates, indispensable when venturing into the world of dream interpretation.

The symbolic experience deeply touches a human being. It allows a person to connect with a dimension that is supra-personal, merging mystery with contemplation. Indeed, each symbol summons meanings and interpretations spanning human history: each evokes deeper possibilities than the visible and speaks a language that, while imperceptible to our physical ears, can be perceived by our spirit. It is something that brings with it a greater and often hidden meaning, all to be interpreted. Anthropological, mystical, historical, theological, and esoteric studies have confirmed, over the course of humanity, that a series of symbolic images have recurred; these surpass time, space, and the individual, conveying a history of the spirit we can understand. This is especially true when such images appear or recur in our dreams, where the unconscious and subconscious communicate with us in secret. Emblematic symbols' presence in our dreams can offer us important messages to help us interpret the needs and potential hidden in a particular moment of our lives.

Getting to know the significance of these symbols is thus the first step we take in exploring the secrets of our interiority, starting with one element that can touch upon broader meaning.

This illustrated book covers three hundred symbols—three hundred constants—coming from many eras and cultures. They are divided into categories, each symbol provided with an analysis of the meanings evoked, not stopping at a psychoanalytic reading but intersecting with information from various disciplines and civilizations.

Azzurra D'Agostino

NATURAL
ELEMENTS

STAR

DESIRE * DESTINY

MEANING OF THE DREAM

A star represents self-knowledge through unconventional intuition, dreams, emotions, and imagination. Imagination is what illuminates and transcends the daily life of existence. It evokes profound desire and a sense of direction.

MEANING OF THE SYMBOL

In the Renaissance, the *governo delle stelle* ("government of stars") denoted unconscious behaviors, just as the expression "written in the stars" refers to a kind of specific destiny. The stars are a guide during travel and influence businesses, born under a good or bad star. For alchemists, the star represented the luminous unity of the self.

SUN

MEANING OF THE DREAM

The most powerful of energies, the highest expression of creative fertility comes to visit us, a sign of the opportunity to know and illuminate our unconscious. Getting too close to these flammable energies is to get lost: to challenge human limitations is to face destruction.

MEANING OF THE SYMBOL

Over the centuries, the sun has been a symbol of sovereigns and rulers, representing eminence and earthly power. But it has also symbolized the light of knowledge and holiness. The all-seeing eye is guardian of the universal order that allows it to prosper with its light and heat.

MOON

INSPIRATION ✳ DARK SIDE

MEANING OF THE DREAM

The moon rises to inspire and lead us back to our mystery. It carries us beyond rationality, reminding us that there is always a side of us that stays dark. It signals a call for our capacity to create magic, to the power of ecstasy, and to the cycle of all things.

MEANING OF THE SYMBOL

This celestial body, which dies and is reborn each month, represents the cyclical and mysterious flow of existence and governs everything wet, from the tides to the human body. As death's scythe, and as the bow with which Artemis hunted, she is both beautiful and terrible. Her thoughtful and haunting nature has inspired artists throughout time.

ECLIPSE

CONJUNCTION * ABANDONMENT

MEANING OF THE DREAM

An eclipse represents the ego obscured by the unconscious, a point where a source of light on our inner depths is blocked. The transitory nature of the eclipse, in which opposites touch each other (sun and moon, darkness and light, day and night) means that the abandonment of light is inevitably followed by its rebirth.

MEANING OF THE SYMBOL

An eclipse signifies lack, cessation, and abandonment. The reign of darkness, even if for a brief moment, has always been considered a dire omen of catastrophic events such as earthquakes, epidemics, or the death of a sovereign.

RIVER

CHANGE ✳ CHANNELING

MEANING OF THE DREAM

A river speaks of life through flow, freedom, dangerous currents, the risk of drowning, and floods, yet at the same time indicates the channeling of the flow of energy in one direction. It teaches us about the passing of things and rebirth.

MEANING OF THE SYMBOL

Rivers are life-giving streams flowing in worlds above and below, along which major human civilizations have developed. All mythologies tell of how the great waters manifested on the earth in the form of a river, an element often considered sacred.

LAKE

MEANING OF THE DREAM

A lake is a mysterious expanse in which we see reality's reflection. The world is suspended and replaced by strange water, only to reappear beyond the shore. The disappearance is well described in the similarity between the words "lagoon" and "lacuna."

MEANING OF THE SYMBOL

In many civilizations, a lake represented the realm of the dead, a place where physical substance is lost in the depths of another world. Mirror of reality, an enchanted space of magical creatures, the lake is the wisdom of the feminine, the need for balance between nature and spirit to assure life.

WATERFALL

BALANCE * SPLIT

MEANING OF THE DREAM

A waterfall splits the landscape. It is a breach whose force flows onto a precipice, creating movement that contrasts with the towering rocks. Its roar balances the silence of the rocky cliffs, and its power reminds us how the immutable is part of a flow in perpetual movement.

MEANING OF THE SYMBOL

A waterfall is considered a flow whose power nourishes the dark realms of the underworld, from which it rises upward to reappear in ours. It is strength, a roar, an abyss, and eternal movement. In China, it represents the element of water in the form of a dragon.

AIR

MEANING OF THE DREAM

When the psychic environment is too closed or suffocating, we feel the need for air to breathe and to clear our minds. Dreaming of this element can signal intuition, imagination, ideation, and abstraction, but also a lack of efficacy and solidity in its volatile nature.

MEANING OF THE SYMBOL

This is the element in which spirits, souls, and divinities dwell. A source allowing life to thrive, fire to burn, and sound waves to propagate. Its pressure can lead to cataclysms like hurricanes and tornadoes. Trembling and magical, it is a source of inspiration that supports the wings of those who fly.

SKY

IMMENSITY ✳ THE DIVINE

MEANING OF THE DREAM

The sky represents unlimited space, the reflection of the infinite in our soul, and the place of the divine par excellence. At night, the flickering stars can be read as sparks of consciousness in the darkness of the unconscious.

MEANING OF THE SYMBOL

In Buddhism, the pure clarity of the sky symbolizes enlightenment in the mind of the Buddha. In many founding myths, the sky is the place of divinities, seat of the king of the gods, who represents cosmic order. Contemplation of the sky returns to us our dimension, our place in the small world.

CLOUD

MEANING OF THE DREAM

The cloud is a key component of man-nature symbolism: think of "storms of emotion," of thoughts that "cloud" the mind, or to live with one's "head in the clouds." Or think of recognizing shapes in them, constituting the background of the psychic process. The cloud is the origin of rain, but it also evokes the possibility of transformation through spiritual practice.

MEANING OF THE SYMBOL

In Mayan cosmology, the demiurge took the form of a cloud, from which he created the universe. Likewise, Allah, according to the Islamic esoteric tradition, before revealing himself existed as an unknowable vapor. In their oscillation between taking shape and formlessness, clouds represent the infinite exchange between the ethereal and the terrestrial.

RAIN

GROWTH ✳ CHANGE

MEANING OF THE DREAM

The rain clears away all that is dark and trapped in an emotional inability to see. When one is in a state of uncertainty, it nourishes the dry earth within. It illuminates and revives what seemed dead and washes away the waste that separates mind, body, spirit, and imagination.

MEANING OF THE SYMBOL

In much of the world's mythological traditions, there is talk of a great rain with which the gods destroy the world before repopulating it. Rain purifies and nourishes the earth, fertilizing it and allowing for life. It demands new perspectives, which keep us safe from the sky's least auspicious signs.

ICE

PETRIFICATION ✳ RESISTANCE

MEANING OF THE DREAM

Ice has an ambivalent meaning. On the one hand, it represents freezing, the petrification of the potentialities of water as a moldable and fertile element, something that traps the dynamism of consciousness. On the other hand, its hardness is a resistance to that which is inferior.

MEANING OF THE SYMBOL

According to Nietzsche, inclement air strengthens the spirit and has the positive value of teaching the rigor of climbing a mountaintop. Let us pay careful attention that the blocking of the transition's symbolic meaning not be excessive, or it will lead to the death of the soul.

WATER

BIRTH * FLOW

MEANING OF THE DREAM

In dreams, water is a symbol of birth, of something coming into the world (a new self, a project). The irreversible movement of water is generally fruitful and nourishing: moving upward it creates rain and dew, and downward streams and rivers.

MEANING OF THE SYMBOL

Water symbolizes terrestrial and natural life, the concrete occurrence of existing and coming into the world. It purifies, smooths, nourishes. It is the emblem of cleanliness par excellence, and for this reason it is present in baptisms and in ablutions prior to rites.

EARTH

MEANING OF THE DREAM

There can be many ways in which the earth appears in dreams: in handfuls, in shovelfuls, it opens up beneath us, or we find it in our mouths. In any case, it has to do with the material issues of life, since the earth is not only the element that sustains us but also the one that feeds us.

MEANING OF THE SYMBOL

Compared with water, earth has the characteristics of firmness and materiality. In some cultures, Mother Earth is a goddess, while the Promised Land is the spiritual center. If affected by an earthquake, it contributes to the general meaning of an abrupt change. According to esotericism, earthquakes in fact arise from the earthly layer of fallen wisdom, and by interacting with human passions, they cause eruptions and tremors.

SEA

WOMB * POWER

MEANING OF THE DREAM

The sea, like all bodies of water, has to do with birth, nourishment, and fertility. Its constant movement recalls the progress of life and our continuous change. Its strength in storms indicates the power of our inner world.

MEANING OF THE SYMBOL

Since the most distant times, the sea has been a border, a place of the unexplored, a mysterious environment full of dangers. For these reasons, it has always attracted pioneers and Argonauts. Its presence symbolizes the womb.

LIGHT/DARKNESS

SPIRITUALITY ✳ INEFFABILITY

MEANING OF THE DREAM

Light is associated with the spirit: indeed, receiving "enlightenment" means reaching a higher spiritual plane. With it appears morality, intellect, and the seven virtues. If darkness appears, we are faced with something not yet manifested.

MEANING OF THE SYMBOL

Light is the emblem of our highest characteristics and historically has always been paired with the obscurity of darkness: one is not humanly bearable without the other. They both have to do with the origin of the universe and life's medley.

DUSK

PASSAGE ✳ SEDUCTION

MEANING OF THE DREAM

The short time that passes between
the fading away of day and the
arrival of night is full of sweetness,
expectation, and eroticism. It is the
daily passage of life and indicates a
transition, an "end of time."

MEANING OF THE SYMBOL

For the Inuit, dusk was the moment when the shaman's shadow sep-
arated from his body to enter, in its transparency, invisible realms. In
popular belief, it is the moment when twilight energies awaken and
dangerous creatures prepare to appear.

MUD

DISSOLUTION ✳ RENEWAL

MEANING OF THE DREAM

Mud can soil and bog someone down, but it also has the potential to be shaped. To cross it signifies being on the way to firmer and drier places. After the dissolution of one state, a new one comes along for the facing.

MEANING OF THE SYMBOL

According to some beliefs, silt is the dust of water, just as ash is that of fire. Ashes and dust create images of definitive transformation of matter, residues of the original elements. They suggest an end, but every end presupposes a beginning.

FOG

AN INDETERMINATE STATE * REVERIE

MEANING OF THE DREAM

Fog causes us to lose our orientation, which is why it symbolizes a less absolute type of knowledge linked to imagination, ambiguity, and nuance. It can be frightening not to know what is in front of you, but by relying on something other than logic alone, we will be able to overcome the uncertain.

MEANING OF THE SYMBOL

According to Scandinavian mythology, the kingdom of the dead was located in a wasteland dominated by frost and mists. In Asian legends, the mist instead represents a state of internal disturbance in which spirits are able to manifest.

SNOW

LETHAL BEAUTY * BLOCK

MEANING OF THE DREAM

The magnificence of snow is cold, far from the touch of man. It creates beauty and fantasies of transformation, but at the same time hides a danger. According to Freud, the presence of snow in a dream represented repressed feelings, "frozen" for protection.

MEANING OF THE SYMBOL

Snow recalls the Platonic ideal of perfect form, transforming the landscape to its basic elements. In many cultures, there are fairies and snow queens, archetypes of beauty but also of potentially lethal ruthlessness. It reflects so much light that, rather than illuminate, it blinds.

NIGHT

MEANING OF THE DREAM

The night has an ambivalent meaning: on the one hand, it suggests a brief death, an absence, an end, and on the other, an epiphany that can occur through contemplation of the starry sky, small lights revealing themselves to consciousness.

MEANING OF THE SYMBOL

According to an Orphic myth, in the beginning there existed Night, a black bird endowed with divinatory powers, that, fertilized by the wind, laid a silver egg from which Eros, the god of love, was born. It symbolizes well the nearness of the dark side to the regenerating powers of enlightenment.

THUNDER

MEANING OF THE DREAM

Thunder awakens our attention from a state of distraction. It announces storms but also transfers energy by setting things in motion. It frees us from the normal noise of existence, reawakening our psyche and liberating our decision making.

MEANING OF THE SYMBOL

For many archaic civilizations, thunder was the voice of the gods or of their personifications. For some peoples, it corresponded to the bellowing of the divine bull, the roar of the magical jaguar, the beating of the thunderbird's wings, or the roar of Thor's chariot wheels. It is a symbol of great physical or emotional shock.

LIGHTNING

MEANING OF THE DREAM

Lightning may be a revelation of an impending disaster, but it is above all illumination. It is a warning, a clarification of a situation that we cannot read clearly on a conscious level. It guides us in following an intuition that we had ignored.

MEANING OF THE SYMBOL

For Hindus and Buddhists, lightning is embodied as a weapon of spiritual transformation that relentlessly demolishes the arrogance of the self. Shamanism knows the mystical experience of a "flash" favoring clairvoyance.

RAINBOW

MEANING OF THE DREAM

It is in the colors of the rainbow that the pact between heaven and earth is implemented. In its continuous dematerialization and regeneration, it denotes change and suggests the process implemented by emotions between what is known and the unknown. It is our bridge: fragile, but with great possibilities.

MEANING OF THE SYMBOL

The Norse legend of Ragnarok describes a rainbow bridge that collapsed under the weight of the giants who came to destroy the earth. In many stories, it is actually a passage for supernatural emissaries and a harbinger of great changes.

FIRE

MEANING OF THE DREAM

Fire is a mediator between opposing forms—between forms in the process of creation and in the process of disappearing, which it is able to determine with its energy in itself. It is the power of heat that heals and nourishes, but if poorly managed, it is the devastating power of a lethal fire.

MEANING OF THE SYMBOL

Many peoples have celebrations linked to fire, from Saint John's fires to fireworks. They symbolize two opposing magical actions: on the one hand to bring about sufficient energy and heat, and on the other to purify and destroy the forces of evil.

SALT

KNOWLEDGE * INCORRUPTIBILITY

MEANING OF THE DREAM

Because of its ability to sterilize and preserve, salt symbolizes that which is not corrupt and what lasts. It is thus an emblem of incorruptibility (of a person, a material, or a situation). At the same time, it represents knowledge that goes beyond mere cleverness.

MEANING OF THE SYMBOL

The Romans were paid in salt rations, and the term "salary" comes from that tradition. It is a precious resource useful for cooking, preserving, and purifying, but which if taken in excessive quantities proves to be harmful.

OBJECTS

KEY

SEARCH * DISCOVERY

MEANING OF THE DREAM

A key represents the tension between restriction and freedom, search and discovery. A key may safeguard treasures, secrets, and truths either dangerous or enlightening. It is a path toward opening to self-awareness, to the heart of a loved one, to the enigma of peace of mind.

MEANING OF THE SYMBOL

The key is a mercurial symbol: it must be sought and tried several times before one is able to open one's enclosed consciousness and one's object of desire. Whoever owns the key becomes the guardian of the threshold.

CUP

PROTECTION * WORLD OF POTENTIAL

MEANING OF THE DREAM

A cup contains liquids, elusive elements that are not easily contained, that signify what is possible. It is a positive sign of something that moves and mixes, which is protected and contained by the vessel. It sometimes also combines with the most sacred power, with mystery.

MEANING OF THE SYMBOL

Especially when equipped with a lid, during the Romanesque period, the cup was identified with the heart. Just as a chest or coffer, it symbolizes a container, a concretization of what surrounds one's center. It protects, holds, and today is still held up, in the sense of celebration and to make a toast.

CROWN

GLORY * RESPONSIBILITY

MEANING OF THE DREAM

The glow of precious gems in a crown still casts a spell over observers today. This speaks to the continued power of its symbolism, representing a glory guaranteed by a noble, ancient ritual iconography.

MEANING OF THE SYMBOL

Over the centuries, the crown has been identified with the sun, emblem of power and divine endowment. It is an object that bears with it a destiny. But beyond its grandeur and ability to empower its wearer, a crown can also be heavy, a harbinger of responsibilities that are very difficult for an individual to manage.

HOUSE

MEANING OF THE DREAM

In dreams, every feature of a house, understood to symbolize one's deepest self, represents our various layers. The facade is our mask, the roof our thought, its openings our body, and its rooms are to be read according to their various functions (such as a need for rest or conviviality).

MEANING OF THE SYMBOL

In mystical traditions, the house represents the female element of the universe, an enclosed place, just like a garden or enclosure. It is the supreme container of wisdom and protector of tradition.

MASK

CONCEALMENT ✳ TRANSFIGURATION

MEANING OF THE DREAM

Each transformation brings with it a mysterious, disturbing atmosphere, since it renders something different from the way it was before yet also remains itself. In this sense, a mask simultaneously hides and transforms. It protects us and gives us new powers in connection with its shape.

MEANING OF THE SYMBOL

In Greek theater and in African religions, a mask facilitates a transition from what you are to what you wish to be. This tendency to metamorphosis is the primary reason, which is enriched on a symbolic level by what the mask itself depicts.

BRIDGE

PASSAGE * DESIRE FOR CHANGE

MEANING OF THE DREAM

If in our dream we cross a bridge or
if we see a bridge joining two pieces
of land, crossing a river, or passing
over a road, a message is being
delivered: we desire a change.

MEANING OF THE SYMBOL

In many traditions, the bridge represents a union between distant
things: in Jewish faith, it is the link between God and his people, in
China it is a conjunction between heaven and earth, and in ancient
Greece it was Iris, messenger of the gods. Thus, for various peoples,
a bridge is what binds the world of the senses to the spiritual world.

STAFF

SUPPORT * TOOL FOR PUNISHMENT

MEANING OF THE DREAM

A staff or cane links to a twofold symbolism that depends on its potential use: it certainly can provide support as we walk along our path, yet at the same time, it is also an instrument of punishment. It can signify our need for support or our need to break up a given situation.

MEANING OF THE SYMBOL

The ancient Egyptians held a celebration connected to the birth of the sun staff. It coincided with that moment immediately following the equinox, in which the increasingly weak sun appears to need a staff to lean on.

CORD

BOND * BELONGING

MEANING OF THE DREAM

In a dream, a cord symbolizes a deep connection. We are linked to something via attachment, affinity, and dependence.

MEANING OF THE SYMBOL

In Hindu symbolism, a silver cord symbolizes the sacred inner path that binds the intellect to spiritual essence. In the form of a rope, it refers mainly to a social significance. Indeed, in monastic clothes or military uniforms, sashes and ribbons indicate to what particular group someone belongs.

WHIP

MEANING OF THE DREAM

The whip, in its many variations, brings together the symbolism of the lasso and the scepter, both emblems of power. It also expresses the possibility of punishment or, even better, of a stimulus, in contrast to the purifying sword.

MEANING OF THE SYMBOL

The Romans bound their whips to their triumphal chariots, and similar tools were used in the cult of Zeus in Dodona. With its power to wrap around and dominate something, in many civilizations a whip symbolizes superiority (of the king, the people, or divinity).

OVEN

FERTILITY ✳ DEATH

MEANING OF THE DREAM

An oven represents an extreme transformation: it reduces wood to ash, but it cooks and provides heat at the same time, nourishing and protecting us from ferocious beasts. It generates and transforms in an ambivalent change passing through death and regeneration.

MEANING OF THE SYMBOL

In Neolithic times, an oven had the shape of a mother's womb, and it navigated the centuries retaining this meaning. It is a place where the deceased are transformed. It carries the ambiguous characteristics of the "terrible mother," as in the traditional fairy tales, where witches are thrown inside.

CAPE

DIGNITY ✳ SEPARATION

MEANING OF THE DREAM

A cape is a feature of elegance that distinguishes its wearer while also being a symbol of separation. It signifies self-control and the ability to emerge. Yet it also evokes a pair of wings, with which we are ready for flight.

MEANING OF THE SYMBOL

In the history of fashion, in all the eras in which it has resurfaced, a cloak has ensured its wearer a touch of superiority. From the bas-relief of the Mithras of Fiano Romano, showing the sacrifice of a bull, to today's superheroes, the cape is a distinctive symbol of special powers (physical, economic, or moral).

SHIP

GUIDE * LIFE

MEANING OF THE DREAM

A ship sailing through our dreams is
a symbol of the body and a vehicle
of existence. If buried underground,
it refers to a hidden and repressed
"second life." If ancient, it represents
ancestors and traditions. If broken, it
alludes to damage (either something
deteriorating or unfinished).

MEANING OF THE SYMBOL

In Mesopotamia, Egypt, Crete, and Scandinavia, the ship was a subject of worship. Traditionally, it is associated with the sun's journey
in the sky and nighttime journey to the sea. The origin of the term
"carnival" refers to a procession of ships (the *carrus navalis*).

GOLD

MEANING OF THE DREAM

Gold represents glorifying light, the sun on earth, and a superior quality is conferred onto any object made of the material. It is also an essential element of a hidden treasure, of something precious that is difficult to reach.

MEANING OF THE SYMBOL

A golden sword symbolizes a perfect spiritual decision. According to Hindu doctrine, gold is a "mineral light." It represents glorification, spiritual assets, and enlightenment. For these reasons, it adorns many spaces related to power and the sacred.

HELMET

MAGICAL POWER * PLUNDER

MEANING OF THE DREAM

Because a helmet was once adorned to convey the possession of magical powers, to dream of one not only evokes protection and strength but also symbolizes our divine power. It is associated with the mystical powers of the head, for which it is shaped.

MEANING OF THE SYMBOL

As one of the first items looted from the enemy, a helmet becomes a crown of the victor. The most extraordinary, original helmets are those that belonged to Japanese samurai of the 16th century; each unique specimen transformed the warrior into a divinity with supernatural powers connected with its decoration: these included forces of nature, animal guides, and auspicious creatures.

PEARL

PRECIOUSNESS
SOMETHING THAT CANNOT BE ERADICATED

MEANING OF THE DREAM

A symbol of virginity and purity, the pearl evokes something priceless and brightly guarded in the depths of our psyche—a teardrop melting the most bitter sadness away with its beauty. At the same time, it also represents a piece of suffering that cannot be eliminated but rather transformed with layers of living substance.

MEANING OF THE SYMBOL

A pearl is a treasure given to brides, a symbol of young love, and an item invested with healing capabilities. Over the millennia, it has symbolized all that is precious or unexpected, the result of an event, or the subject of a search.

SWORD

CONNECTION ✳ FREEDOM

MEANING OF THE DREAM

The sword is a symbol of a wound, suffered and inflicted, and in this sense, it is associated with freedom and strength. At the same time, its makeup of a hilt and blade renders the sword an emblem of connection, especially when it assumes the shape of the cross.

MEANING OF THE SYMBOL

In stories from ancient China, a city's founders carried swords. A sword was believed to chase away evil spirits by the Romans and the Scots. Accompanied by fire and flame, it promises purification and is used in magical dances.

MIRROR

MEANING OF THE DREAM

A mirror's meaning is ambivalent: it is a symbol of consciousness as well as a reflection of the world. We find the mirror disturbing, with its power to create a double. It may be a portal opening to another world, which is why mirrors are covered in certain circumstances.

MEANING OF THE SYMBOL

In fairy tales, a mirror often has magical powers that summon creatures and apparitions and bring back images it has absorbed from the past. A lunar symbol for its passivity and its ability to change from "empty" to "inhabited," a mirror symbolized the multiplicity of the soul to prehistoric peoples.

STONE

LONGEVITY ✳ WISDOM

MEANING OF THE DREAM

Something written in stone represents something that lasts, a knowledge that overcomes the passage of time. Stone's immutable hardness is opposed to the brevity of life. The philosopher's stone is thus a symbol of supreme wisdom.

MEANING OF THE SYMBOL

Stone has always been part of human life, since the construction of the first tools. Some stones from the rest of the universe have become pilgrimage destinations, like the Black Stone in Mecca, which has been described as a meteorite. Various peoples believed that the souls of ancestors resided in stones.

COFFIN

LOSS * NEW LIFE

MEANING OF THE DREAM

An emblem of death, a coffin represents not only loss but also preparation for rebirth into new life. This second facet is well exemplified in fairy tales describing glass coffins with an element of the feminine inside (a maiden asleep).

MEANING OF THE SYMBOL

When ritual cremation was practiced, the deceased were contained in vessels or baskets. The construction of coffins took place later, to protect from predators and evil spirits.

MEDICINE

CARE * DIFFICULTY AT HAND

MEANING OF THE DREAM

Medicine is an elixir that protects and provides solutions (to a physical problem or, symbolically, a situation). It also represents something difficult to ingest, which can make people feel ill prior to healing—the difficulty we must experience in order to reach a solution.

MEANING OF THE SYMBOL

Mankind has always sought remedies for its ailments within nature, sometimes also finding them in the ambivalent power of certain objects or people. Consider the thaumaturgic touch of a king, or hangman's rope, which was said to have healing properties.

POISON

MEANING OF THE DREAM

Stingers, poisonous liquids, snakes with a lethal bite: poison can appear in a dream in many forms.
It represents a feeling of danger, of risk, which causes fear. Yet at the same time, it contains in itself a death to be experienced, in order to free up a still-latent change.

MEANING OF THE SYMBOL

Poison has the same qualities as the *pharmakon*, which translates to "pharmaceutical"—a drug, a medicine, or a potion. These substances are characterized by the same properties: they can be lethal if taken in an excessive dose but are remedies when well calibrated.

DRUM

MEANING OF THE DREAM

A drum not only provides rhythm but also interacts with the heartbeat of all things, according with or modifying it. It represents our need to move forward in agreement with the rhythms of the world or to make our own felt. Given the shamanic power attributed to a drum, it is also a tool for exorcism (of fears or destructiveness).

MEANING OF THE SYMBOL

It is an instrument of shamanic healers but also a means of communication between tribes. The first drums date back to the Neolithic period and were given the role of counteracting natural disasters, something that was believed in for many centuries.

BELL

MEANING OF THE DREAM

The shape of a bell recalls the wisdom of the void, and its toll is able to call us to our deepest spirituality. It marks the time, but only at salient moments that call for our attention. A bell's toll anticipates an announcement.

MEANING OF THE SYMBOL

According to an ancient Russian myth, the tolls of a bell have the power to keep our hearts from destructive intentions or to rouse feelings of repentance. Bells have always announced news of victory and celebration.

TRUMPET

ANNOUNCEMENT ✳ CALL

MEANING OF THE DREAM

From troops' call to arms to angels' tidings heralding an extraordinary event, even the apocalypse, the trumpet is a symbol of that which captures our attention. The dream signals that we should notice something extraordinary happening.

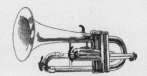

MEANING OF THE SYMBOL

In Western traditions, the trumpet appears via many depictions of sacred texts. It is the instrument of angels, prophets, and priests. Rows of men would play a trumpet upon a ruler's arrival, and it is an instrument of Jewish ritual for relating events that are sacred or relevant to the community.

COLUMN

ENERGY * ASPIRATION

MEANING OF THE DREAM

Standing in temples in strength and grace, the pillar unites sky and earth in an act of human commitment. It symbolizes all the strength and vital energy needed to "support" a situation or other people, but it also encourages us to lift our eyes toward heaven, reminding us that we can lift ourselves from what oppresses us.

MEANING OF THE SYMBOL

According to many traditions, ascetics—and the Stylites in particular—took refuge in meditation on the top of a pillar. This kept them in proximity to the sky, detaching them from everyday distractions.

BATHTUB

MEANING OF THE DREAM

The washing of one's body not only signifies physical well-being and self-care but also a moment of profound renewal and transformation. It is an abandonment of the old self heralding the birth, in us or in our relationships, of something new, all yet to be created.

MEANING OF THE SYMBOL

Many religious rites involve the immersion of one's body in water, from Christian baptism to the ritual washing of indigenous Americans. Here cleanliness, as an inner purification, is close to godliness or devotion.

CRADLE

SECURITY ✳ LIFE'S BACK-AND-FORTH

MEANING OF THE DREAM

We find the continuous rocking of a cradle reassuring. An emblem of the "second" mother's womb that welcomes the newborn after birth, it evokes a sense of safety, rest, and protection. Each swing echoes the direction of life, with its ups and downs—for which we perform rituals urging the Great Mother's protection.

MEANING OF THE SYMBOL

The cradle is a complement to the coffin: one leads into life, the other carries us toward the afterlife. Our culture was born in the fertile plain between the Tigris and the Euphrates, dubbed the "cradle of civilization."

BED

MEANING OF THE DREAM

The bed and the bedroom are ambivalent places where we take refuge for rest: we depart the rhythm of everyday life, seeking quiet and serenity, but we are also in contact with darkness, with nightmares, with the supernatural. It is the space where one's person surrenders to the vulnerability of the self.

MEANING OF THE SYMBOL

The romantic French term "boudoir," connoting the bedroom in certain contexts, derives from the word *bouder*, to "sulk" or "shun." Indeed, it was the place ladies could retire from the company of others and be alone with their own private thoughts.

BROOM

MAGIC * LUST

MEANING OF THE DREAM

A broom transforms an environment by removing dust. Its rhythmic movement evokes in us an image of its autonomy that is almost diabolical, linking it to witchcraft. It thus recalls the fickleness, lust, and the darkest sides of the psyche.

MEANING OF THE SYMBOL

In Zen Buddhism, the broom is a symbol of wisdom, sweeping away delusion, opposing that which confounds awareness. In popular tradition, it is rich in arcane energy, halfway between humble daily occupations and magic.

CARPET

DILIGENCE * BALANCE

MEANING OF THE DREAM

The complexity of the work required to weave a carpet renders it a symbol of diligence and dedication to a project. Its ability to fly in Middle Eastern tales also alludes to the balance—physical and internal—necessary to direct one's imagination over everyday living.

MEANING OF THE SYMBOL

Legend has it that the first Persian garden carpet was commissioned by King Khosrow I in the sixth century. In many religions, it serves as a templum, that is, a sacred space separate from the profane world.

GLASS

TRANSPARENCY ✳ FRAGILITY

MEANING OF THE DREAM

A glass lightbulb represents this
material well as a sign of clarity,
knowledge, and vision. If we manage
further illumination of its light, we
become transparent to ourselves.
At the same time, this element's fragility
reminds us that everything can, if not
handled correctly, reduce itself into
small, sharp fragments.

MEANING OF THE SYMBOL

Invention of the technique of glass blowing dates to the first century
BC, in territories corresponding to present-day Syria. For millennia,
people have shaped objects in this lasting, odorless, beautiful material. For alchemists, it was the emblem of transformation.

CHAIR

MEANING OF THE DREAM

The chair represents our position in life: if we place ourselves at the edge, it can signify hesitation, as well as anticipation or a readiness to react. Our body's posture indicates whether we are relaxed, formal, or authoritative. To see someone "enthroned" indicates the ruling principle. It symbolizes the potential unity of the individual.

MEANING OF THE SYMBOL

The chair in its most regal form, the throne, is often a feature of the divinities, a place where something transcendent sits, a symbol that embraces everything. Whoever sits on it possesses the gifts of divine wisdom and strength.

TABLE

DELIMITATION * COEXISTENCE

MEANING OF THE DREAM

Around a table, one makes decisions. One meets for work or convivial settings with friends and relatives. It is a defined place where you can also sit alone waiting for someone "else," but it can also signify enjoyment of one's own peace.

MEANING OF THE SYMBOL

The table of King Arthur's knights was round, as was the Solar Table of the Orphic Mysteries, a symbol of perfection. In contrast, a table with corners creates tension between different competing places arranged according to a hierarchy. It remains a powerful tool for inclusion or exclusion in any type of meeting.

LAMP

IDEA ✳ INTROSPECTION

MEANING OF THE DREAM

If a light is turned on in our dream and its source is not a natural one, it represents the dawn of an idea, a subtle form of epiphany. It has to do with the brilliance of the psyche and its authentic path toward wisdom.

MEANING OF THE SYMBOL

The Greek philosopher Diogenes carried a lamp with him in his symbolic search for an honest man. The term "lamp" derives from a Greek root that means "shining" or "illuminated." It is mingled with hope, freedom, or the possible creation of a spark.

STAIRS

MEANING OF THE DREAM

A dream of taking many steps on a staircase signifies reaching different levels of awareness (of oneself or a situation). It symbolizes both sublimation upward and attachment to foundations, life's highs and lows, and the risk of overconfidence.

MEANING OF THE SYMBOL

From the Latin *scandere*, meaning to ascend, a staircase chiefly presents the idea of an ascent, an instrument that elevates us from a position or a situation by gradual steps. It is, however, also possible to see a perspective of descent, with various levels toward the depths.

WINDOW

LIBERATION * OPENING

MEANING OF THE DREAM

Dreams and patterns are timeless windows into the complex movements of our inner world. They represent a transparent threshold that opens a passage and allows you to look beyond, freeing something locked up or repressed.

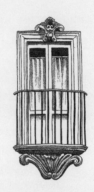

MEANING OF THE SYMBOL

The term "window" derives from the ancient Icelandic *vindauga*, or "wind" and "eye." In civilizations around the world, a window was opened upon a person's death to let loose the soul toward immortality.

LOCK

PROPERTY * CONSTRAINT

MEANING OF THE DREAM

Locks are symbols of ownership, wealth, and secrets. To dream of locking doors for repressive purposes, much like keeping everything indiscriminately unlocked, is a symptom of incorrect use of protective mechanisms. Breaking a padlock may represent a necessary use of force in order to change a situation.

MEANING OF THE SYMBOL

In Mali, the lock symbolizes union between husband and wife, and it denotes a system requiring that specific limitations be respected. What is traditionally kept under lock and key says much about our fears and routine attitudes.

PHONE

CONNECTION ✳ WARNING

MEANING OF THE DREAM

A phone is very common in contemporary people's dreams, being one of the most widely used items in everyday life. It can constitute a call from the psyche, between its desires and conflicting attitudes, and a warning from consciousness that is good to heed.

MEANING OF THE SYMBOL

A phone is a tool for connection, which cannot exist if no network or person on the other end can be assumed. Its ring immediately catches our attention, while the response is highly varied, depending on the interlocutor we speak with.

UMBRELLA

PROTECTION * SUPERSTITION

MEANING OF THE DREAM

As an age-old instrument that protects us from the weather, from too much sun or rain, the umbrella represents an imaginary filter between personal and interpersonal spheres. It offers shelter to the ego from the showers of the psyche and negative energies that surround us.

MEANING OF THE SYMBOL

The umbrella is traditionally an object of superstition. For example, it is said that an umbrella should not be given as a gift, just as one should avoid opening one in enclosed spaces, as it is thought to unleash the "storms" of unfortunate events.

SHOE

MEANING OF THE DREAM

In dreams, shoes can represent the characteristics of one's point of view and indicate how authentic it is. If the shoe is new, it can mean a new beginning. If it is uncomfortable, it means that we are in a stagnant situation in need of renewal.

MEANING OF THE SYMBOL

Shoes have often had divine or magical connotations, from the winged sandals of Hermes to seven-league boots. For centuries, shoes have represented social status, while in many sacred traditions the removal of shoes signifies a rejection of the riches of lay life.

APRON

OCCULT POWER ✳ NOURISHMENT

MEANING OF THE DREAM

As the typical garment of cooks, artisans, and artists, an apron evokes a power to transform elements, a secret wisdom that not everyone can master. It was also a feature of sorcerers and alchemists. Precisely due to its traditional pairing with work in the kitchen, it suggests a nourishment that is ever-present.

MEANING OF THE SYMBOL

In France, a Venus figurine made of bone dating back to 25,000 BC was found with carvings depicting an apron or skirt at the hips. This dating suggests that the apron was likely the earliest human garment.

RING

MEANING OF THE DREAM

The enclosed form of a ring,
recalling the eternal circle, renders
it an emblem of a bond, a pact,
a promise, or a vow. Its shape
implies stability and containment.
It can even represent subservience
(alluding to those who wear a ring in
connection with divine power).

MEANING OF THE SYMBOL

The origin of a ring worn on one's finger dates back to Greek mythology, when Prometheus was freed from his sentence by Zeus and was forced to wear a ring made from the chain that had bound him. It often is given magical attributes in folklore and represents both love and power.

EARRING

MEANING OF THE DREAM

Among many peoples, this adornment indicates a rite of passage, especially for women and girls, or a transition to a fertile age. For men, on the other hand, it symbolizes a statement of one's individuality. In combination with the ear, it also symbolizes spiritual hearing.

MEANING OF THE SYMBOL

In some cultures, the earring has religious value, especially in the East, where it is connected to the acceptance of spiritual wisdom. For ancient Mesoamerican populations, it was a sign of penance, with its connection to the piercing of flesh.

NECKLACE

PROTECTION ✳ CHARM

MEANING OF THE DREAM

In dreams, a necklace can carry various meanings, depending on its value. If it breaks, it symbolizes a need to bring an end to a relationship with someone, or even warns of risking the loss of something precious. Stealing a necklace symbolizes the desire for an authentic bond with oneself.

MEANING OF THE SYMBOL

A necklace as embellishment also has the meaning of protection, safeguarding the link between the head and the rest of the body. In myths, it is traditionally an attribute of female deities, highlighting their beauty and charm.

GARLAND

CYCLICAL NATURE OF LIFE ✳ FORCE OF RENEWAL

MEANING OF THE DREAM

With its circular, intertwined, continuous pattern, a garland recalls the eternal development of things, affirmed in the perishable materials from which it is constructed. This is precisely because plants also contain the powerful spirit of nature, which is always germinating life anew.

MEANING OF THE SYMBOL

In different civilizations, the garland sits on the heads of athletes and immortal poets touched by the inspiration of Apollo, god of spring. Christ's crown of thorns was to mock his "royalty" on the part of those crucifying him.

HAT

METAMORPHOSIS ✳ CODE

MEANING OF THE DREAM

A hat can reveal or hide what a person truly is. It can imply a transformation from an individual to a member of a group, as with sacred headdresses or contemporary sports teams. It is part of an expressive code indicating specific intentions (like taking off one's hat, begging for alms).

MEANING OF THE SYMBOL

The hat has not only the function of protecting one's head from weather events but also of revealing secret facets of an individual. The god Mercury wears a winged hat, a symbol of the volatility of the vital spirit.

VEIL

HIDING ✳ REVELATION

MEANING OF THE DREAM

A veil has the purpose of protecting us from something we are not ready to comprehend. When we manage to lift one of its edges, a deeper, more elemental knowledge is revealed. The psyche, in the sometimes-dark forms it takes in our dreams, veils or unveils itself in paradoxical ways.

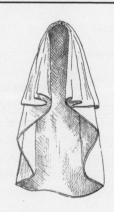

MEANING OF THE SYMBOL

The veil has carried profound political and religious meaning since ancient times. It indicates belonging, chastity, protection, and even virility for the Tuareg people, for example. In some philosophies, the material world is a veil that hides true reality.

SCISSORS

TRANSFORMATION ✳ LIBERATION

MEANING OF THE DREAM

Scissors are a symbol of transformation: they cut off what is no longer needed, thus representing the power of freedom to express, liberate, or cut away what is in excess. At the same time, they remind us that the life of consciousness is subject to cuts and fragmentation.

MEANING OF THE SYMBOL

In myth, the power to cut is often guided by a supernatural objective. Consider, for example, Atropos, the third of the Greek Fates, who cuts the thread of life, in a gesture opposite to the cutting of the umbilical cord. In popular culture, scissors are a tool to injure and to castrate.

COMB

BRINGING ORDER ✳ GIVING SHAPE

MEANING OF THE DREAM

A comb, modeled on human fingers running through one's hair, symbolizes the creative power to shape the ideas of one's consciousness. It detangles the wild nature in us, lending order to things and ideas. Dissolving knots, lightly touching, and caressing it evokes the power of Eros.

MEANING OF THE SYMBOL

In some cultures, the comb is not only a practical item but also a talisman with magical powers. A Siberian shamanic myth tells of a woman in flight who tosses a comb behind her; this conjures a forest that offers her protection.

MONEY

WEALTH ✳ ACTIVITY

MEANING OF THE DREAM

Money symbolizes material wealth and the imaginary wealth of the psyche. The ability to access these treasures depends on our activity and propensity to save, spend, or squander.

MEANING OF THE SYMBOL

Money implies circulation, exchange, and activities, as well as loss and debt. The Akan peoples of West Africa would forge golden spirit and animal figures in stone or metal, and for thousands of years, coins with the depiction of a king or deities have been made, symbolizing specific powers and energies.

BAG

MEANING OF THE DREAM

One must pay attention to the circumstances under which the bag appears in dreams: lost, found, disorganized, open, or closed. Generally, it points to the containment or removal of elements of identity, from money (psychic energy) to sexual impulses. Stealing a handbag corresponds to a transgression.

MEANING OF THE SYMBOL

Prior to the existence of pockets, men and women carried leather bags that attached to their belts. These later became a symbol of bank officials, merchants, and tax collectors.

BASKET

MEANING OF THE DREAM

Basket weaving relies on symbolic designs that express the unity between nature, ancestral experiences, and spiritual teachings. It is a common container for the spontaneous gifts coming from the natural world, evoking abundance and the eternal cycle.

MEANING OF THE SYMBOL

An Easter basket full of eggs represents spring's promise of rebirth, and the same symbolic assumption is incorporated in the picnic basket. A basket implies stories of tradition, such as those in the Bible, protection, and regeneration of body and spirit.

NET

TRAP * CONNECTION

MEANING OF THE DREAM

The symbolism of a net is twofold. On one hand, it is an emblem of being reigned in, trapped (by physical or inner ties). On the other, it signifies the interconnection of all things (which is also in the contemporary concept of a network).

MEANING OF THE SYMBOL

The ancient Sufi imagined the capture of the divine using invisible nets. Christ told his disciples to become "fishers of men." In many mythologies, a net connotes an organizing power that transforms contrasting energies.

CHAIN

MEANING OF THE DREAM

The first meaning that a chain evokes is that of such a connection that is so inextricable as to almost constitute coercion. To dream of breaking a chain, on the other hand, can signify liberation or a freeing of oneself from a relationship or situation that felt oppressive.

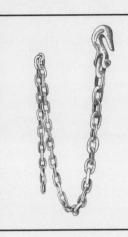

MEANING OF THE SYMBOL

Chains represent the weight of events that to us seem irreparably linked. The metal from which they have been forged, like lead, linked to Saturn, invokes the alchemists, who imagined chains that could connect different levels of existence.

SCALE

MEANING OF THE DREAM

On a symbolic level, this precision tool for measuring weight indicates a balance between opposites: head/heart, matter/spirit, conscious/unconscious. If a scale appears in our dream, it reveals a need to bring harmony into situations or relationships.

MEANING OF THE SYMBOL

Traditionally, the scale is an attribute of blindfolded justice. The Kabbalah claims that before creation, there was a scale of the universe from which all opposites were born. A motif of the "weighing of souls" in the afterlife is found in many founding civilizations.

COMPASS

MEANING OF THE DREAM

The design of a compass precisely lays out a separation and distinguishing of internal and external. An emblematic tool of precision and science, it indicates a need to resort to rationality. In an even broader sense, a magnetic compass symbolizes our path and a need for orientation.

MEANING OF THE SYMBOL

In the Middle Ages, a compass was the attribute of the divine architect, who reestablished the act of the cosmos's creation by composing a circle, with God at the center point.

CALENDAR

TRANSITION ✳ PREDICTION

MEANING OF THE DREAM

The calendar positions our life relative to a series of periodic processes, organizing time, something otherwise difficult to divide in terms of the eternal. It signifies stages, transforming symbolic deaths and rebirth into transitions, and promotes prediction, lending regularity to the undefined.

MEANING OF THE SYMBOL

All calendars attempt to give order to time and eternity, from the Aztec calendar engraved in stone to the lunar cycles followed since the Assyrians and Babylonians, to the twelve-year cycle of the Chinese zodiac based on animal symbolism.

WHEEL

MOBILITY * ROUTINE

MEANING OF THE DREAM

Any element referring to the wheel takes us back to the mobility of the psyche and our advancement. However, depending on the situations in which it appears and the feelings it transmits to us in the dream, it can also communicate regression and routine.

MEANING OF THE SYMBOL

The Wheel of Fortune in tarot symbolizes the twists of fate, and it alludes to the power of the wheel: a fundamental discovery for humanity and a symbol of progress, with the capacity to contain magical energies, as well as a means of torture and of labor.

HAMMER

STRENGTH ✳ CAPACITY TO MOLD

MEANING OF THE DREAM

Dreaming of a hammer can carry a twofold meaning, depending on its context—on the one hand, a violent force giving into an impulse, on the other, an ability to direct the will and imagination to carve out valuable works or to build new processes and forms.

MEANING OF THE SYMBOL

Well-known is the Norse god Thor's hammer, a fundamental tool for defeating evil forces that threatened the earth. In many civilizations, the creators of cosmic order use a hammer to give shape to creation.

FIREARM

MEANING OF THE DREAM

To dream of weapons, and firearms especially, presents us with our fears of giving in to violence, of not being able to control aggression. This is our dark side that presses us and seems unknown to us. On the other hand, not pulling the trigger symbolizes a capacity to control one's awareness.

MEANING OF THE SYMBOL

In popular festivals, shooting blanks has been a method for removing evil spirits. The power that firearms provide, for hunting, war, defense, robbery, or many other violent means, has been a topic of debate for centuries.

BOW AND ARROW

ASCENT ✳ HITTING A TARGET

MEANING OF THE DREAM

To dream of a bow and arrow connects us to someone far away who needs to be reached through elevation, through flight. It binds us to a target in a dynamic tension, amplifying the limits of our ego as we attempt to achieve our goal.

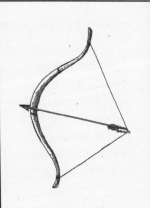

MEANING OF THE SYMBOL

From the Paleolithic period onward, a bow and arrow have symbolized one's rise. Hunting becomes a metaphor for desire, which then allows someone to hit and penetrate a target, be it that of one's true self or of love. The bow and arrow evoke not brute force but concentration: consider the stories that contain formidable archers as protagonists.

AXE

VIOLENCE * NEED FOR WISDOM

MEANING OF THE DREAM

Symbolically, the axe has a dark side, constituting the most violent tool when used for heinous crimes. It is the weapon of an executioner, the blade of the guillotine. It recalls the need to handle one's strength with care and skill, considering well the objectives being addressed.

MEANING OF THE SYMBOL

In Tibet, the axe is emblematic of the clean break that must be given to all negative tendencies of the mind. In the Congo, an axe depicted the union of male and female in the king's authority. In the Roman Republic, it was a symbol of lawful authority.

BICYCLE

LIGHTNESS * BALANCE

MEANING OF THE DREAM

The bicycle is an emblem of light-heartedness, lightness in speed, autonomy, and the ability to easily reach places other forms of transportation cannot. It is also a symbol of the need for practice to find one's balance and avoid dangerous pitfalls.

MEANING OF THE SYMBOL

The bicycle became widespread and popular during the nineteenth century, a period of extraordinary discoveries and inventions. It played an important role in the elimination of the corset and bodice in female fashion, thus becoming an instrument of women's emancipation.

ANCHOR

CONSTANCY ✳ HOPE

MEANING OF THE DREAM

Even amid a storm, something within you is able to keep you safe. Never fear. Insist that, with tenacity, you will be able to reach the world beyond the open sea.

MEANING OF THE SYMBOL

The anchor, as a symbol of the sea, is widespread in many cultures. In Christianity, combined with the letters alpha and omega, it represents eternal hope. In other traditions, its crescent arm is associated with the female principle, and its shank, above, to the male principle: it is the union from which life is created.

BODY

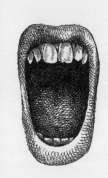

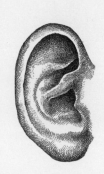

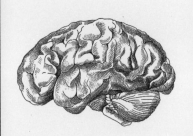

TEETH

AGGRESSION * TREASURE

MEANING OF THE DREAM

Using our teeth, we symbolically bite into life morsel by morsel for survival and growth. Grinding your teeth, showing them, is a sign of anger and aggression.

MEANING OF THE SYMBOL

In ancient times, the lack of even a single tooth blocked one's ability to become a priest, as perfect teeth were likened to moral integrity. The Maya adorned their teeth for ritual purposes with jewels and shells. In magic, the tooth also constitutes a form of treasure, as told in legends of tooth fairies or mice who bring coins to children.

BONES

IMMORTALITY * DEPTH

MEANING OF THE DREAM

A bone seen in a dream indicates the arrival of our most intimate and deepest part, the essence, our secret heart. It is the marrow of hope, the possibility of life within that appears to have dried up. It represents the immortal part of us.

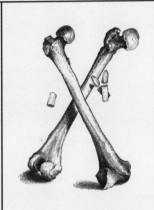

MEANING OF THE SYMBOL

Bones represent the essential starting point for the reanimation of the dead in mythological conceptions. The hunting peoples of the Arctic regions avoid breaking the bones of animals and reassemble them in burial in order to obtain their forgiveness.

EYE

COGNITION ✳ VISION

MEANING OF THE DREAM

The eyes represent lucidity and are the emblem of understanding. But when we dream that they are set into different parts of the body (the hands, chest, or other places on the head), they signify an ability to see into the beyond.

MEANING OF THE SYMBOL

Since the ancient Egyptians, the eye has been associated with the sun, the light of spirit, and intelligence. Two eyes express a physical and spiritual normalcy, and the "third eye" indicates superhuman knowledge. A single eye is associated with superhuman powers of destruction (like that of the Cyclops).

HAIR

MEANING OF THE DREAM

The presence of hair in a dream firstly evokes vital energy, spiritual and physical strength, and power. If dark, it symbolizes earthly energy, blonde or light hair symbolizes the sun, and auburn hair Venus. Thick hair represents spiritual evolution, while dreaming of losing it indicates failure.

MEANING OF THE SYMBOL

In some religions, entering a monastic order involves shaving one's head, which simulates the rejection of earthly goods and passions, a path toward an absolute ascetic practice.

FEET

MEANING OF THE DREAM

The foot, as is the hand, is one of the two essential parts in symbolizing man and his soul. In particular, the foot is the person's support. It also indicates, as a footprint, someone leaving, figuratively or literally.

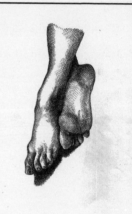

MEANING OF THE SYMBOL

The importance of the foot as a solid basis for standing is highlighted in Greek mythology by the negative characteristics associated with characters who have a deformed foot. Likewise, the most vulnerable point of an invincible figure is found in the foot, like the heel of Achilles or Krishna.

BODY MARKINGS AND ALTERATIONS

EMPHASIS * TALISMAN

MEANING OF THE DREAM

Marks on the body highlight certain elements and their characteristics, whether distinctive signs of beauty or indications of imperfection or fault. Tattoos symbolize belonging, one's definition, or a talisman that favors and protects.

MEANING OF THE SYMBOL

Anthropologists have confirmed the use of tattoos in many cultures, often used in rites of passage or generally in moments when the personality transforms. They also indicate possession, as if they were a mystical black mark.

SPIT

ALLIANCE ✳ CONTEMPT

MEANING OF THE DREAM

Spit represents a way in which a pact is sealed, one less noble than blood yet symbolizing a promise to which one is to be faithful. At the same time, we spit on something we deem unworthy of our respect. It can also signify the need to "spit out" what we have kept ourselves from saying.

MEANING OF THE SYMBOL

Like other body fluids, saliva was considered a magical liquid by many peoples. In Norse mythology, Kvasir, a being so wise that there was no question he could not answer, was born from the saliva of gods.

TEARS

REDEMPTION ✳ EMPATHY

MEANING OF THE DREAM

Tears shed by others provoke a
reaction of relief, empathy, and
consolation. Their emergence, for
any reason of joy or pain, represents
a moment of purification that
frees the body and mind from
sedimented impurities.

MEANING OF THE SYMBOL

Tears best express their power in folklore: they free someone from
a curse or heal parts of the body where they fall. This is taken up in
many myths from various traditions, from India to ancient Greece.

MOUTH

EXPRESSION * FUSION

MEANING OF THE DREAM

The mouth manages to reveal, just through its expression, the way in which we "swallow" what happens to us. It is the means through which we nourish ourselves and with which we symbolically "devour" the other through the most sensual kisses.

MEANING OF THE SYMBOL

The oral cavity is a cavernous space that humanity has filled over the centuries with fantasies and myths. From Krishna, who, as a child, contained the universe in the back of his throat to Indian deities who emerged from the mouth of the lord of creation to the Cyclops of the Odyssey who devour Ulysses's men.

EXCREMENT

CREATIVITY * WILL

MEANING OF THE DREAM

The presence of feces in a dream symbolizes methods to contain creative impulses: from a "blockage" of something that cannot or does not want to emerge to the anomalous release of out-of-control energy when we cannot hold it back.

MEANING OF THE SYMBOL

Excrement has always been highly regarded for its fertilizing properties, not only for fields but also from a metaphorical perspective. This is synthesized in the Aztec word for "gold," which also meant "divine excrement."

NOSE

MEANING OF THE DREAM

Smell, which connects our consciousness to emotional parts of the brain, is the privileged channel of access to our past and to primordial qualities, like the recognition of a suitable partner. It is an emblem of selection: from the discarding of poisonous foods to the attitude of those who "turn up their noses" snobbishly.

MEANING OF THE SYMBOL

The Egyptians believed that the breath passing through the nostrils of a goddess could bring a deceased king back to life. For this reason, the nose was treated with great care during mummification, recognizing its central value.

ILLNESS

SUFFERING * TRANSITION

MEANING OF THE DREAM

Illness is primarily experienced as suffering, morbidity, or discontent. It expresses a moment of weakness and crisis, or the need for renewal. In this sense, it can also be considered a significant passage, a transformation toward another self.

MEANING OF THE SYMBOL

Prehistoric peoples identified the painful experience of illness with the loss of the soul, the violation of a taboo, a privileged relationship with spirits, and the aptitude for shamanism.

ASHES

CONCLUSION ✳ THE ESSENTIAL

MEANING OF THE DREAM

Something reduced to ashes represents a definitive conclusion, the irrevocable, be it the remains of a love, a destroyed building, or a body. It can lead to remorse and humiliation. At the same time, it also symbolizes the essential, a concluded process brought to its end.

MEANING OF THE SYMBOL

Ashes symbolize immortality, self-sacrifice, and destiny purified in the austerity of fire. To absorb the qualities of the deceased, Indian ascetics sprinkle their bodies with funerary ashes taken from a sacred bonfire.

KNEE

MEANING OF THE DREAM

The knees symbolize our flexibility, which, if used with awareness, allows us to be stable at the center of existence. It is precisely for this reason that kneeling represents obedience and submission to forces recognized as greater than ourselves: a divinity, an enemy, love.

MEANING OF THE SYMBOL

In Indo-European languages, "knee" is akin to the word for "generate." This fulcrum, allowing us to make the most of our movements, in fact contains a liquid that in ancient times was considered our lifeblood.

LEG

MEANING OF THE DREAM

Legs are associated with our journey of life. They lead us, not only metaphorically, toward the achievement of our goals. Legs marching forward symbolize cohesion. Legs and feet "planted firmly on the ground" are synonymous with practicality and rationality.

MEANING OF THE SYMBOL

In military iconography, chained legs are a symbol of submission and defeat, unlike those portrayed on the march. Foot races have always been a key event in the Olympic Games, highlighting their role in our survival.

LIVER

HIGHLY INTENSE EMOTIONS ✳ PURIFICATION

MEANING OF THE DREAM

The liver has the function of purifying the body of waste and also of violence and anger. It was once considered the source of the most intense emotions, and for this reason, it had divinatory properties. Dreaming about it evokes our need to express hidden feelings.

MEANING OF THE SYMBOL

According to Plato, the purpose of the liver was to reflect the images of the rational soul, and for this reason, it could also be a way of predicting the future. It was from this concept that the art of haruspices developed (from *ar*, or liver, and *spicio*, to look).

HEART

MEANING OF THE DREAM

The heart is a living symbol that conveys similar meanings as the sun: the power center and the main source of life, courage, and strength. As such, it can be pierced by cupid's arrows or broken by a rejection.

MEANING OF THE SYMBOL

In the ritual sacrifices of Mesoamerican peoples, the still-beating heart was offered to the god of the sun. Even in Christian iconography, the heart of Christ, as an object of veneration, is depicted in flames or with a crown of thorns, symbolizing Christ's sacrifice.

BLOOD

LIFE * REVENGE

MEANING OF THE DREAM

Blood is the center of our embodied life, and its symbolism in our feeling of its sacredness is immediate. Linked to images of violence, it symbolizes a threat of revenge or a need for purification.

MEANING OF THE SYMBOL

Templars and other heroes sealed their bonds in blood. The Maasai drank the blood of lions, the Vikings that of bears, and warriors that of killed adversaries, signifying how greatly this vital liquid embodies the essences and central qualities of individuals.

BREAST

MEANING OF THE DREAM

The duplicity of breasts symbolizes the opposing meanings that they embody, depending on whether the breast, symbol of life or death, is offered or denied. It represents the divine spark from which comes the nectar of nourishment, the elixir of life, immortality, and wisdom.

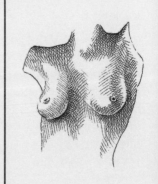

MEANING OF THE SYMBOL

Associated with lunar and feminine properties, the dual nature of breasts also indicates a form of passage from known to unknown. Its capacity for erotic attraction is a link to the magico-religious elements of the divine. It is an expression of strength.

NAIL

SURVIVAL * FIGHTING

MEANING OF THE DREAM

Claws and nails are emblems of the conflictual relationship we sometimes have with others and of the harshness of natural selection, albeit in social terms. They connect us to our animalistic and predatory side.

MEANING OF THE SYMBOL

Thanks to the power they constitute in a fight, nails and claws are protective talismans in many cultures. Over the centuries, long nails have been associated with regression into the dark powers of the unconscious, and it is for this reason that witches, sorcerers, and vampires have these features.

FINGER

MEANING OF THE DREAM

The fingers are a part of the hand's creative force and symbolize its greatest power. They are what shapes our action. They are the instrument and the emblem of the relationship between the internal and external world.

MEANING OF THE SYMBOL

Michelangelo depicted all the divine power to spark life in the index finger of God, extended toward Adam. In palmistry, it is not only the opposable thumb—one of the human being's fundamental attributes—but each finger that represents a person's individual characteristics.

ARM

CONNECTION ✳ ACTIVITY

MEANING OF THE DREAM

The arm is our primary connection with the world, from the primordial gesture of bringing food to our mouth to raising a trophy as a sign of victory. It symbolizes the ability to act and the activity itself, also nurturing our relationships in the embrace.

MEANING OF THE SYMBOL

In Egyptian hieroglyphics, the pictogram showing an arm was a generic indication of activity, doing, or action. For a long time, it was a key unit of measurement, together with the hand and the foot.

NECK

MEANING OF THE DREAM

The neck brings the head and body together in not only a literal sense but also a metaphorical one. It is a vulnerable element, especially in the throat, and given its connecting function, it is involved in psychic conflicts. When something gets "stuck in our throat," or makes our throat "tighten," it provides a physical manifestation of an internal imbalance.

MEANING OF THE SYMBOL

In kundalini yoga, the throat is the fifth of seven chakras and symbolizes the empty and pure space in which all elements combine.

TONGUE

MEANING OF THE DREAM

The tongue not only serves to distinguish flavors and decide what is healthy or not for us but, above all, has the enormous power to allow for words and expression. In this sense it can be constructive or destructive, as in slander and gossip.

MEANING OF THE SYMBOL

All the creative and destructive power that this corporeal element symbolizes is emblematically contained in the threatening language of the gorgon Medusa.

BEARD

INTELLECT * ANIMALITY

MEANING OF THE DREAM

The beard is a symbol of virile strength, the ability to reason, and good use of the intellect. In parallel, however, there are shadows it evokes: the devastating strength, savagery, or loss of control of Bluebeard or of demonic creatures.

MEANING OF THE SYMBOL

The beard, framing the mouth and jaw, has long been associated with the power of *logos*, and for this reason, philosophers were always depicted with beards in ancient Greece. In some historical moments, it became a form of protest against dominant models.

EAR

INTUITION * RELATIONSHIP

MEANING OF THE DREAM

Dreaming of an ear extended by
or toward someone solicits the
thought that the person deserves
our listening and attention.
Hearing, more than any other sense,
promotes deep understanding,
based on intuition.

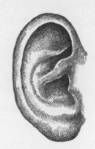

MEANING OF THE SYMBOL

A form of meditation involves listening to external sounds. Hindu
cosmology refers to a primal murmur that can be heard through
deep inner concentration. Furthermore, the ear ensures our essential sense of balance.

BRAIN

ESSENCE * MYSTERY

MEANING OF THE DREAM

The brain symbolizes something containing the greatest mystery— that of who we are and that of a higher mind binding the reality of all things together. It is considered a space of thought and consciousness, and as such able to contain the essence of a person.

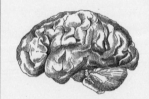

MEANING OF THE SYMBOL

In ancient times, the brain was considered a mysterious place that, if controlled, could express itself in infinite ways, and for this reason, an enormous power was attributed to it. In some civilizations, such as in ancient Crete, or in Jewish Kabbalah, it was considered sacred.

HEAD

IMMORTAL SOUL ✳ LIFE FORCE

MEANING OF THE DREAM

Since ancient times, the head has represented the seat of incorruptible life, fertility, and the psyche. It is the place where life is generated, but the skull cautions of its demise.

MEANING OF THE SYMBOL

The Headless Horseman is destined to wander tormented for eternity, and thus images of decapitation in history and in the imagination remind us of incompleteness, as in all civilizations it is believed that the head contains the essence of who we are.

SPINAL COLUMN

FORTITUDE ✳ STABILITY

MEANING OF THE DREAM

The spine is necessary for the human being's posture in life, both effectively and figuratively. It represents the essential strength of one's mind in bearing the weight of an authentic life, uniting high and low, providing structure, and representing something that is lasting and stable.

MEANING OF THE SYMBOL

One of the most important symbols in Egyptian hieroglyphics was a pictogram in the shape of a tree or spine. It meant "lasting" or "stable" and symbolized the resurrection of the pharaoh into eternity and the stability of the kingdom.

HAND

ACTION * GIFT

MEANING OF THE DREAM

It is time to act: to collect fruits, gifts, changes. This is not a waiting phase but one of doing.

MEANING OF THE SYMBOL

Hands connect thought to action: they greet, guide, care, divide, caress. For this reason, they have always been central in all kinds of ritual gestures, magical, social, or religious. To wash your hands, for example, represents purification from sin in many cultures, while the fingers of the deceased were considered to hold extraordinary powers and were used in witchcraft.

ANIMALS

DOG

LOYALTY ✳ TRUE PATH

MEANING OF THE DREAM

The dog represents all that eternally accompanies us: our true nature—in perennial balance between the animal and the rational—and death. With his constant presence, a dog guides us toward the path that belongs to us through the realms of the afterlife.

MEANING OF THE SYMBOL

The dog's friendly and benevolent presence has accompanied humans since prehistoric times, both in everyday life and in the imagination. Anubis, the Egyptian god of the dead, was depicted in canine form and judged the deceased by placing their heart on one plate of a scale and a feather on the other. In many other myths, a dog represents a guardian demon of the underworld.

GOAT

PASSION ✳ OBEDIENCE

MEANING OF THE DREAM

If a goat appears in your dream, it means that a period governed by wildness and by passion is on the way. A sheep appearing, on the other hand, is a sign referring to the obedience and strength of the group.

MEANING OF THE SYMBOL

In the Norse tradition, the goat was associated with concepts of protection, power, and fertility. In the Judeo-Christian West, a negative exception was assigned to this figure, making it a symbol of wild unpredictability and whim. The sheep and the lamb are contrasted with the goat as emblems of sacrifice and spiritual purity.

GRASSHOPPER

DESTRUCTION * CHAOS

MEANING OF THE DREAM

The appearance of a swarm of grasshoppers or locusts in your dream symbolizes a situation marked by chaos: in life, they will interrupt harmful and unfortunate relationships and concerns. They can also symbolize a sense of guilt.

MEANING OF THE SYMBOL

In the Jewish tradition, locusts are a force of destruction, to the point of constituting one of the ten plagues God inflicted upon the Egyptians, who were guilty of not having freed the Jews from slavery. The same symbolism has been handed down in Christian culture. In the Book of Revelation, they are portrayed as coronated knights, sent to earth to torment humans.

HORSE

INNER FORCE * MOVEMENT

MEANING OF THE DREAM

When a horse bursts into your dream at a gallop, it is a manifestation of life's eternal movement and the need to progress. It also embodies the pairing of life and death, as well as one's divinatory capacity.

MEANING OF THE SYMBOL

Symbol of the wind, sea-foam, and light, in the Vedic text of the *Brihadaranyaka Upanishad,* the horse has a cosmic significance that draws on its movement, evoking the eternal onward continuation of existence. In Western tradition, the horse corresponds symbolically to the sign of Gemini. The belief that a horseshoe brings luck derives from this animal's magical character.

SWAN

REALIZATION OF DESIRES ✳ UNION OF OPPOSITES

MEANING OF THE DREAM

The appearance of a swan in our dreams is identified with the appearance of an archetype that speaks to a lunar beauty and a bond between opposites. It is also a symbol of melancholy, passion, and pleasure fulfilled in itself.

MEANING OF THE SYMBOL

A positive figure, able to lead us beyond life and death with its song, the swan was dear to Venus, goddess of beauty and love. Its immaculate whiteness harkens back to the concept of an honest nakedness, while its phallic neck and soft body instead represent supreme union or the realization of our highest desires.

SEASHELL

BEAUTY ✳ BIRTH

MEANING OF THE DREAM

With the characteristic sound we hear bringing it to our ear, a shell represents the call of the tide's flows, at birth and rebirth. It allows for a pulling back in intimacy and the ability to reveal oneself gradually.

MEANING OF THE SYMBOL

Since ancient times, the seashell has evoked feminine charm and mystery. Its image is often linked to that of Venus, whom the Greeks believed was born from a shell. In early Christianity, the empty shell represented the rise of the soul toward immortality.

SNAIL

SELF-SUFFICIENCY ✳ HIDDEN VITAL POWERS

MEANING OF THE DREAM

Dreaming of snails recalls our desire to take refuge in a safe place and then re-emerge just as they do at dawn, with the dew, and in the rain.

MEANING OF THE SYMBOL

The silver spiral of its shell is associated with the lunar cycles, to such a degree that the Aztecs depicted their god of the moon enclosed within a spiral shell. Many cultures are fascinated by their reserved nature, one containing, however, a vital essence with the capacity to combine male and female. The shell snails always carry with them renders them a symbol of self-sufficiency.

DOVE

INNOCENCE ✳ HOPE

MEANING OF THE DREAM

Emblem of beauty, simplicity, and docility, the dove is a sign of individual and collective hope. Indeed, doves symbolize the arrival of good news and peace in situations of conflict.

MEANING OF THE SYMBOL

In ancient China, the dove was associated with longevity and filial piety. For the Egyptians, doves were winged messengers. Great mothers like Aphrodite and the Syrian Atargatis took on the appearance of the dove, a quintessential bird of love given its monogamous nature. For alchemists, it acts as a mediator between our noble aspirations and the whirlwind of life.

DOLPHIN

MEANING OF THE DREAM

Dreaming of a dolphin symbolizes being rescued. These creatures keep us company in the lonely passages of life and bring us to safety when our own means go under.

MEANING OF THE SYMBOL

The presence of a dolphin in a dream indicates a submerged force that can guide us toward what is right for us at that moment. In fact, it has been found that dolphins can apparently attune themselves to our energy fields, restoring their balance when altered. As emissaries from the womb of the ocean, they bring us messages from the deep.

ELEPHANT

STRENGTH ✳ WISDOM

MEANING OF THE DREAM

In a broad sense, an elephant's appearance in dreams evokes the power and strength of the libido. Yet its round shape and gray color at the same time connect to the weightlessness of clouds and the mythical idea that they can create them.

MEANING OF THE SYMBOL

The elephant is a pivotal figure in Indian tradition, which describes them as caryatids of the universe, as the mount of kings, as winged creatures, as axes of the world, and as mountain peaks. In the Middle Ages, the concept of the elephant spread as an animal sign of wisdom, temperance, and eternity.

BUTTERFLY

BEAUTY ✳ REBIRTH OF THE SOUL

MEANING OF THE DREAM

The beauty of the butterfly is one of the most emblematic images of psychic self-renewal, giving us the capacity to overcome the greatest of traumas.

MEANING OF THE SYMBOL

Australian Aborigines identified butterflies with the spirits of the deceased returning to earth. To the Aztecs, they represented the heroic soul of sacrificed enemies. The ephemeral nature of their existence and their attraction to light make butterflies a symbol of the potential destructiveness of passion, and a butterfly's inconstant shadow evokes the instability of desire.

ANT

INDUSTRIOUSNESS *
CONNECTION TO THE COMMUNITY

MEANING OF THE DREAM

The presence of an ant speaks to us
of the importance of care for others
and the dignity of doing, calling
attention back to imperceptible
realities, yet full of strength and
power.

MEANING OF THE SYMBOL

The ant is a sacred animal in various cultures, including some Native
American cultures. The community element is central, as is an inspiration to a physical, psychological, and spiritual diligence. In the
myth of Cupid and Psyche, the latter passes a test with the assistance
of ants, which represent the element of earth.

ROOSTER

LIGHT ✳ RESURRECTION

MEANING OF THE DREAM

A rooster appearing in our dream tells us of how good provides protection from evil and the light saves us from darkness. Just as he, with his morning crow, celebrates the overcoming of night's shadows, we can trust the sun that always rises.

MEANING OF THE SYMBOL

For his fiery red feathers and crow, proclaiming and reaffirming the existence of things each day, the rooster was devoted to Apollo, god of the sun. In Indian and Pueblo Native American mythology, it was also associated with a return to light and life. In Christianity, the rooster is a symbol of resurrection.

CAT

FORTUNE * SUBVERSIVE POWER

MEANING OF THE DREAM

Feline energies are fertile and positive: to dream of cats protects us from the destructive gnawing of our mind. As a familiar of witches, however, they also have a darker aspect to them.

MEANING OF THE SYMBOL

Their elegance and intelligence meant that cats were assigned the roles of guiding figures in many ancient fairy tales and legends. In Japanese culture, they are considered wise spirits who bring luck; depictions of them are found everywhere. It was in medieval times that the figure of a cat was associated with witchcraft and darkness, to such a degree that they were quickly classified as demons.

CRAB

MEANING OF THE DREAM

The movement of a crab recalls all that is variable, temperamental, or inconstant, from feelings to decisions. At the same time, the crab's shell encourages a tenacious defense of ourselves from intrusions, helping us to see clearly the place that is our "home."

MEANING OF THE SYMBOL

In Western astrology, Cancer dominates the fourth house of domestic life, where the sign oscillates between a need for solitude and the desire to share. Mythological stories of giant crabs carrying ships away signify the reversals that can come from the depths.

GOOSE

MEANING OF THE DREAM

In a manner similar to the swan's, this bird's appearance is a beneficent one, connected to the Great Mother and the descent to the underworld. Its homonymous "Game of the Goose" represents this symbol well; it is related to fate, collecting the dangers and fortunes of our existence.

MEANING OF THE SYMBOL

Present in many folkloric tales—from those of the Brothers Grimm to *The Wonderful Adventure of Nils* by Nobel Prize–winner Selma Lagerlöf—the goose acts as a magical salvific element and is often the hero's guide on his journey.

FROG

WISHES FOR THE FUTURE ✳ PURIFICATION

MEANING OF THE DREAM

When a frog comes jumping into our dream, it represents a sign of future well-wishes and the birth of new projects or a new self. An aquatic, lysergic creature, the frog brings us a message of purification and fertile possibility.

MEANING OF THE SYMBOL

The blue-glazed ceramic frog—perhaps in the form of an amulet or as a gift of new-year well-wishes—came to us from ancient Egypt. This animal was dear to the god Khnum, who shaped human life with his potter's wheel. In many cultures, the frog is a harbinger of purifying rains and is central to shamanic rites.

EAGLE

HEIGHT * POWER

MEANING OF THE DREAM

The eagle symbolizes an ability to fly high and is thus identified with the sun and the spiritual principle. It is an evocation of origin, in contrast with the owl and other night birds of prey, which express an end.

MEANING OF THE SYMBOL

Associated with divinities of power, the eagle can be depicted with the head of a lion, its earth-bound equivalent. It is an emblem of lightning and of war. Both in the East and in pre-Columbian America, it represents the celestial principle fighting against the netherworld.

155

HEDGEHOG

WISDOM * CULTURE

MEANING OF THE DREAM

The appearance of a hedgehog in our dreams symbolizes the presence of or need for wisdom: not simple intelligence, but actual applied, considered knowledge that allows for conscious common-sense choices. It also symbolizes culture with the capacity to teach.

MEANING OF THE SYMBOL

In many traditions, the hedgehog is considered so wise that it assisted God during creation. In Romanian, Bulgarian, and Latvian cosmogonies, the hedgehog helps the Creator find a way to make space for the waters on earth and in exchange is given its coat of needles.

LION

ROYALTY * HEROISM

MEANING OF THE DREAM

Within the human psyche, the lion is associated with the concept of royalty connected to power, majesty, and dominion over others. It corresponds with qualities connected to heroism and to struggles with strength, value, dignity, and nobility.

MEANING OF THE SYMBOL

The image of the lion was connected to that of the sun and its principles of vital, irrepressible strength, with the capacity to create and destroy. In Western mythology, sun/lion attributes were identified with cosmic forces that replaced the bull/moon duality, which dominated the oldest legends.

FOSSIL

CONCLUSION ✳ METAMORPHOSIS

MEANING OF THE DREAM

The significance of the fossil in a dream is similar to that of stone, the lasting material symbolizing eternity. This case, however, is of something that was once living, thus denoting the end of a relationship, a situation, or our inner state—something that, despite revealing itself as concluded, will continue to carry importance for us.

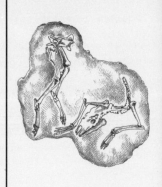

MEANING OF THE SYMBOL

The fossil has always represented a powerful connection between life and death: it opens and stimulates reflection on time made eternal, converting something living into stone.

FEATHER

MESSAGE ✳ LIGHTNESS

MEANING OF THE DREAM

Feathers, with their sensitivity to the slightest wind, represent our ability to grasp the most hidden currents of life; following them, we can draw on new possibilities. As a component of wings, feathers evoke the idea of messengers, whether they be angels or birds.

MEANING OF THE SYMBOL

An emblem of flight and lightness, feathers were used by the Maori to decorate sacred sticks for accompanying the deceased to the kingdom of the gods. Shamans considered them an element of connection between earth and sky.

BEAR

POWER ✳ REBIRTH

MEANING OF THE DREAM

The bear is an extremely powerful symbol, one evoking an ability to courageously face, and overcome, death. The fact that this animal hibernates links its image to the potential for rebirth. It also connects to the maternal facets of nature.

MEANING OF THE SYMBOL

In shamanic societies, initiates had visions in which the bear, understood to be a spiritual animal, tore skeletons into pieces, purified them, then reconstructed them by replacing their old structures with a new one that could endure the most powerful forces.

WOLF

WILD SIDE ✳ DANGER

MEANING OF THE DREAM

The arrival of a wolf in our dream has a twofold meaning: it warns us of a danger yet also indicates the need to resort to the wild in us, to trust the salvific skills that lay in the wildest forces of our unconscious.

MEANING OF THE SYMBOL

In various founding legends, like the city of Rome's, it was a wolf that kept guard over the birth of a new civilization. This demonstrates the importance of ferocious energies lying beneath the surface during the creative process and the construction of something new.

PEACOCK

MEANING OF THE DREAM

The elegance of a peacock that appears in a dream asks us to place our confidence in two things. On the one hand, in the power of extravagance, of trusting in unexpected solutions and originality. On the other hand, its infallible sight and the many "eyes" of its tail remind us that there are other ways to see, apart from our gaze.

MEANING OF THE SYMBOL

The peacock has been associated, like the Phoenix, with the powers of light by virtue of its brilliant plumage. It was thought to have an ability to transform snake venom into medicine thanks to its "eyes of wisdom."

CROW

DISORDER * OPPORTUNISM

MEANING OF THE DREAM

The crow and the raven, with their raucous calls and the dark plumage, represent a disturbing presence, something rowdy and disquieting. Their malice and ingenuity, which lead them to steal and use their beaks to dismantle and to build, signify opportunism.

MEANING OF THE SYMBOL

The two crows belonging to the Norse god Odin—Huginn, meaning "thought," and Muninn, or "memory"—traveled through all the various worlds to scavenge for the truth hidden beneath the surface and bring its messages to the god's ears.

FLY

UNPREDICTABILITY ✳ DISORDER

MEANING OF THE DREAM

A fly has trajectories that make it difficult to catch, and it therefore represents an element we cannot control. Its buzzing around decomposed material likewise teaches us not to escape disorder but to face it, and to make of it something fertile.

MEANING OF THE SYMBOL

For the Egyptians, the fly was a symbol of the tenacity every good soldier was expected to show, to such a degree that a golden fly was used as a military badge. Mosquitoes were associated with healing powers, and shamans wore a mask with their likeness to suck away evil.

BEE

PLEASURE * WISDOM

MEANING OF THE DREAM

Unlike those of ants, the industriousness and ingenuity of bees lead to the production of honey, which has always been considered a precious asset connected to earthly pleasures. Their ingenuity and the complexity of the processes they perform also make them the emblem of ancient knowledge.

MEANING OF THE SYMBOL

In the rites of mystery religions, honey was poured on the tongues and hands of initiates to represent purification of the sun god, making processes of new life and transformation possible.

COCKROACH

MEANING OF THE DREAM

The cockroach has been associated with filth and poverty, but its deep symbolic meaning is connected to the activation of old complexes or regressions. It has the characteristics of resistance belonging to something foreign that seeks to ensure its permanence. It represents the continuity of those who adapt to everything, up to the most extreme disturbances.

MEANING OF THE SYMBOL

The typically Western aversion toward this insect was historically strengthened by the fact that it does not care for light. In African popular stories, it is depicted as a cunning hero of the oppressed.

SPIDER

TRAP * DISMEMBERMENT

MEANING OF THE DREAM

The spider's web refers not only to bonds, fetters, or something that in its bare visibility attracts and ultimately traps us. It also heralds the dismemberment of the self, which takes place when we remain stuck in a spiderweb of unpleasant situations or irritations, such as ambitions and passions.

MEANING OF THE SYMBOL

Ovid associated the grace and ferocity of the spider with Athena. In fact, when the girl Arachne dared to challenge her in the art of weaving, she was, without mercy, transformed by the goddess into a spider and forced to spin for all eternity.

SCORPION

SURVIVAL CAPACITY * TRANSMUTATION

MEANING OF THE DREAM

With its origin at the dawn of time and its inclination toward the dark, the scorpion represents a penetration of dark sides from which one still re-emerges safe and victorious. Although its attack may be fatal, the scorpion is associated with the harvest, fertility, and the possibility of transmutation.

MEANING OF THE SYMBOL

The alchemists called the moment when metals changed to gold the time of the scorpion, calling upon the powerful symbolism of this animal that within itself unites the acts of letting go and becoming.

WHALE

ABYSS * COMPASSION

MEANING OF THE DREAM

Whales represent an ability to descend into the abyss. They are also associated with self-awareness, compassion, and linguistic expression, thanks in part to scientific discoveries demonstrating these qualities. This creature of the seabed enters our dreams to bring us a song from the deep.

MEANING OF THE SYMBOL

Inuit whalers visualized the female soul and that of the primordial whale as a single entity. These were connected to such an extent that the hunt was encouraged by the shamanic trance of the women who remained on land.

FISH

AWARENESS ∗ INNOCENCE

MEANING OF THE DREAM

Fish symbolize our effusion from an archaic and unconscious world, and this is why in many fairy tales a gold ring is found in the mouth of a fish. They signify the innocence of the soul, a luminous dart into the depth of the psyche.

MEANING OF THE SYMBOL

For many archaic religions, divinity lay at the bottom of the sea. Even in Christianity, Christ is represented symbolically as a fish, described as a "fisher of men," as are St. Peter, the Buddha, and Orpheus. Their ever-open eyes recall the eye of God, which sees all.

CROCODILE

PROTECTION ✳ ASCENDENCY OF LIGHT

MEANING OF THE DREAM

Dreaming of a crocodile is not an omen of violence or aggression, but rather a sign of protection and spirit of initiation. Its temperature, which depends on the environment and leads it to warm itself in the sun, embodies the rebirth of light.

MEANING OF THE SYMBOL

According to the ceremony for weighing the heart of the deceased—a tradition of ancient Egypt—a monster with a crocodile head, the body of a hippopotamus, and a lion's mane and paws would devour those who did not correspond to measures dictated by the lord of the order of the cosmos.

SNAKE

HIDDEN FORCE * HEALING

MEANING OF THE DREAM

We find the appearance of a snake disturbing, but its symbolic meaning is very deep, representing death and rebirth. It is a hidden force, a dark and cold one, but one that also can absorb heat stirring beneath the surface, performing the miracle of care and healing.

MEANING OF THE SYMBOL

Considered sacred by the divine Greek healer Asclepius, the snake is the spirit of the doctor, so much so that, even now, depicted entwined with a staff, it is used as a symbol of pharmaceutical care.

MONKEY

MEANING OF THE DREAM

A spiteful and unbridled monkey invading our dream symbolizes the possibility of an instinctive expression free from convention. When especially pernicious, it becomes an emblem of perversion.

MEANING OF THE SYMBOL

In Mayan mythology, the monkey was the only creature that survived destruction. In India, however, it was venerated as a deity of justice and commitment. With Christianity, it became a symbol of lust and greed. Meanwhile, in the modern age, it also expresses the truths of evolutionary theory.

FOX

INTELLIGENCE ✳ CAPACITY TO VIOLATE BOUNDARIES

MEANING OF THE DREAM

The fox is a symbol of cunning and a broader intelligence to overcome the boundaries of what is considered legitimate. It knows how to lose its tracks in the snow by erasing them with its tail and hides its scent by jumping onto the backs of sheep. The fox is thereby able to survive in any condition, and this is its message.

MEANING OF THE SYMBOL

The fox has a central role in Japanese folklore, so much so that in medicine there is a syndrome unique to Japanese people called Kitsunetsuki syndrome. People suffering from this illness believe they have been possessed by a fox.

KANGAROO

A JUMP ✳ DEVELOPMENT OF WHAT WE CREATE

MEANING OF THE DREAM

When a kangaroo jumps into our dream, it announces a leap in our awareness or existence. It also brings us the message that we will need, and know how, to care for and feed what we give to life, whether it is a project, a choice, or a new awareness.

MEANING OF THE SYMBOL

In Aboriginal mythology, it was the kangaroo that reached the center of the continent to cover it with caves, streams, and rocks, which became sacred places infused with creative energy. The red that permeates the sky at dawn is, according to legend, a kangaroo skin placed over the sun to cover it.

RABBIT

MEANING OF THE DREAM

Its easy disappearance into a den
and reappearance in the glow of
twilight has turned this tender
animal into a symbolic guide
on the paths of love leading to
immortality, a superior knowledge,
and our regeneration, which is also
represented in the rabbit's fertility.

MEANING OF THE SYMBOL

According to the Asian legend of the moon rabbit, a Brahman who
had been lost and was dying of hunger asked some animals for help.
The rabbit, moved to compassion, decided to throw itself into the
fire, offering itself as a meal. The Buddha honored the animal's gen-
erosity by casting its image onto the moon.

MOUSE

ADAPTATION ✳ INVISIBLE POWER

MEANING OF THE DREAM

The dream appearance of a mouse nibbling signifies being freed from the knots within our subconscious. It represents all those invisible, even unconscious powers involved in the overcoming of obstacles. Beyond this, the real capacity of mice to adapt calls upon our own abilities to change and survive, even in hostile circumstances.

MEANING OF THE SYMBOL

Emblems of fertility, mice—white mice especially—are also a symbol of wealth, abundance, and luck, as the year of the mouse indicates in Chinese astrology. A mouse shown with the Hindu god Ganesh represents the mind and all its desires.

BAT

THE UNCONSCIOUS * ORIENTATION

MEANING OF THE DREAM

The black wings of bats represent the ambivalent darkness of the psyche, which often inspires unmotivated fears in us. Yet its ability to orient itself in the dark highlights the fact that, relying on a new form of inspiration, we can come upon unexpected resources.

MEANING OF THE SYMBOL

Bats are associated with the forces of the various lunar phases and spirits, and therefore to witchcraft practices. Bloodsucking bats in Central and South America also evoke the mysteries of death and our fears of man-animal hybrids.

COW

PATIENCE * AFFECTION

MEANING OF THE DREAM

The cow is the very image of calm, placidity, and care. Her quiet presence, and her milk, from which some of the most basic foods on our table derive, provides reassurance and encouragement. The massive body of a bull, on the other hand, calls back to the earth element.

MEANING OF THE SYMBOL

For the Egyptians, the Milky Way was formed of a celestial cow's milk. In India, the cow is a sacred animal and is venerated as an entity that can offer protection from every kind of evil.

PIG

INGENUITY * SENSITIVITY

MEANING OF THE DREAM

The idea that pigs are filthy animals is well-established. In actuality, however, they are highly intelligent beings of a deep sensitivity, with a capacity to communicate with humans. A pig's appearance in a dream may suggest that one pay more attention to qualities beyond appearances.

MEANING OF THE SYMBOL

There are many ancient mythologies that envisage the presence of pigs among the divinities. Their symbolic meaning can be briefly traced back to the concept of the unfamiliar, but also those of wealth and fertility.

WORM

HUMILITY * REGENERATION

MEANING OF THE DREAM

The modest, underground work of worms, earthworms, and larvae is a powerful and transformative activity, one that can regenerate the earth and lead it to new life. Thus, these beings are brought to us as a gift in a dream, with an awareness of the importance of humility.

MEANING OF THE SYMBOL

Like the fly and the grain of sand, the worm in the Christian tradition represents the smallest of places eternity resides. Alchemists associated it with a stage in which excessively mature patterns collapse, beginning a phase of renewal.

TURTLE

WISDOM * ORIGIN

MEANING OF THE DREAM

Turtles' longevity and slow and protective nature, with their strong shell in which they can take refuge, have made them a symbol of wisdom.

MEANING OF THE SYMBOL

In many cultures, the turtle is considered custodian of a primal knowledge that surpasses time: a knowledge from which we descend and with which we are able to make contact. There are many traditions tracing the birth of all animals to the turtle, from Iroquois legends to Hindu sacred texts to Chinese beliefs. Several mythological stories connect it to the Great Goddess, to fertility, and to the aquatic and lunar elements.

EGG

ORIGIN ✳ SIMPLICITY

MEANING OF THE DREAM

The egg symbolizes the beginning, the origin of all things, and the source from which events, people, worlds, and moods are descended. Dreaming of an egg stimulates our creativity.

MEANING OF THE SYMBOL

Its simple form, containing the greatest mystery—life—has made the egg a prominent icon in many cultures. According to several indigenous cosmogonies, the world originated from an egg just waiting to be hatched and set life free. In the Christian tradition, its symbolism of birth and origin is accompanied by that of resurrection.

SCALES

DEFENSE * NETHERWORLD

MEANING OF THE DREAM

The robustness of scales is akin to that of a shield, which can defend from something or can oppose resistance. Dreaming of scales evokes the netherworld, a part of us that we do not recognize, but with which we must come to terms.

MEANING OF THE SYMBOL

Many mythological creatures are depicted as covered in scales: dragons, mermaids, and fantastical animals like snakes with canine heads or monsters. But it is not always necessary to look so far away: our skin also has scales. When we experience conflict, and when our energies seek to emerge but are blocked by fear or guilt, scales then appear.

DEER

RENEWAL OF SPIRITUALITY

MEANING OF THE DREAM

Don't allow yourself to be afraid of falls and losses. Entrust to the strength of the Spirit and believe in purity and in renewal.

MEANING OF THE SYMBOL

A stag's antlers, which extend like branches and regrow each year, bind this animal to the symbolism of the tree of life and to the meanings of rebirth and renewal. In many cultures, the deer is seen as a mediator between heaven and earth and thus conveys favorable meanings: the ancient Greeks recognized it to have mystical qualities, while in the Middle Ages, it symbolized heightened religiousness.

VEGETATION

TREE

MEANING OF THE DREAM

The tree represents the completion of work that progresses from desiccation to regrowth. It is a place under which repair can take place. Its crown of branches symbolizes the conjunction of opposites heaven and earth. Meanwhile, fruits, flowers, and birds constitute an expression of the enlightenment we might attain.

MEANING OF THE SYMBOL

In Norse mythology, one root of the cosmic tree plunges downward to reach the source of wisdom and memory, with the other reaching the home of the gods. The tree is a central symbol in alchemy, symbolizing the intensity of inner life.

LEAF

MEANING OF THE DREAM

The growth, fall, and reappearance of a leaf relates to us all the power of existence. Not the simple adornment of branches, it is a living element that provides color and joy. Its appearance within a motif made up of an ensemble represents groups of people and symbolizes the community.

MEANING OF THE SYMBOL

One of the eight ordinary symbols in Chinese tradition, the leaf is an emblem of happiness. It also constitutes societal protection, evoking the fig leaves that Adam and Eve sewed together to cover their nudity. It transforms light into nourishment.

POMEGRANATE

UNITY ✳ FERTILITY

MEANING OF THE DREAM

The pomegranate was a symbol of veneration to goddesses considered the source and regeneration of life, and to dream of its many seeds thus symbolizes fertility (of ideas, projects, etc.). It also represents the majestic forces of the unconscious you stumble upon in embracing the seeds of the self.

MEANING OF THE SYMBOL

The dominant symbolism of this fruit is that of a perfect alignment of the multiple within a sense of unity. Indeed, already in the Bible, it symbolizes the unity of the universe. Since the ancient Greeks, its seeds and pulp have signified the eternal renewal of life in the world.

CORN

PROSPERITY * FERTILITY

MEANING OF THE DREAM

If a corncob appears in our dream, it signifies the existence of great wealth and prosperity in our inner life or in the situation being symbolized. Maize seeds represent the fertility of the earth.

MEANING OF THE SYMBOL

Corn, like almost all grains, has over the centuries carried a spermatic significance, as a fruitful element of civilization and the earth. Peruvians have depicted this symbolism in female effigies made of corn stalks.

APPLE

ORIGINAL SWEETNESS ✳ LOSS

MEANING OF THE DREAM

Iconically, the apple is a fruit of ambivalent symbolism. It represents both the perfect place, as a fruit of paradise, and the loss of original purity of innocence, entailing a symbolic reversal of fate.

MEANING OF THE SYMBOL

Welsh legends recount a journey made by Merlin and Arthur in search of the Isle of Apples, Avalon, from the Welsh afal, meaning "apple." It was said that the holy grail was hidden there, making the island the paradisiacal place of immortality. The apple exists in our imagination both as the forbidden fruit of the Bible and as the poisoned apple in folkloric tales.

MUSHROOM

THE UNEXPECTED * MAGICAL ACCESS

MEANING OF THE DREAM

Symbolically, the mushroom represents something that arrives or pops up unexpectedly, perhaps something that has been working underground, proliferating in the invisible. Its psychotropic powers make it an emblem of special, magical access to the subtle layers of reality.

MEANING OF THE SYMBOL

Many mushrooms are considered sacred in different populations, from South America to Siberia. Shamans use them to strengthen the body and encourage trance states. In legends, they belong to the fairies, who dance and capture men inside mushrooms, which have grown in a "fairy circle."

MANDRAKE

ANESTHETIC * POTION

MEANING OF THE DREAM

If in our dream we see this plant, with its humble appearance, it communicates to us that the element or subject connected to it is operating as a potion, a facilitator, or something to catalyze our energy. This may be erotic or instinctual, but it could also be anesthetizing.

MEANING OF THE SYMBOL

The method of preparing drinks with mandrake, whose properties have been known since Roman times, evokes a need to extract magical content from the depths and resort to fierce energies far from our everyday mental state.

ROOT

MEANING OF THE DREAM

As in a philosophical tree, with roots sinking into the sea or the sky, so our conscience develops, transforming itself with a plantlike structure, drawing nourishment from the unconscious. The root also asks us to hold fast to our deepest nature.

MEANING OF THE SYMBOL

Popular customs include the belief that edible roots have special properties, such as igniting the passions. They are important subjects in Japanese art and underscore how any form of life, even the most humble, can attain enlightenment.

IVY

DEPENDENCE ✴ STRENGTH TO PROTECT

MEANING OF THE DREAM

A vine winds itself around the boundaries of our dream: typically, we associate ivy with this group of tenacious and parasitic plants. What it recalls symbolically is an aspect of the feminine, to do with a force requiring protection. Something in us seems fragile but instead has the power to ascend to heaven.

MEANING OF THE SYMBOL

Ivy was considered sacred by the Phrygians, who used it to pay homage to their god Attis. A stylized ivy leaf was depicted in eunuch priests' tattoos.

FRUIT

MEANING OF THE DREAM

Fruit traditionally symbolizes the properties of an egg, viewed as the primary perfection giving rise to all things. A fruit as the fulfilled state of a flower, containing in its seed the possibility of new life (of projects, experiences, relationships, etc.), speaks to us of realization and earthly desires to which one can aspire.

MEANING OF THE SYMBOL

In the history of humanity, fruits have always traditionally represented fecundity, fertility, and resurrection. Certain fruits appear in Renaissance paintings with allegorical connotations, such as the strawberry, an emblem of paradise.

ALMOND

SACRIFICE ✳ UNION OF OPPOSITES

MEANING OF THE DREAM

The almond symbolically depicts the place of intersection between the circle of heaven and that of the earth, of spirit and matter. In this sense, it therefore represents all forms of dualism. It also evokes a sacrifice, what we let go in order to create space for what rises anew through our creative force.

MEANING OF THE SYMBOL

The symbol of an upright almond was used to indicate the spindle of magical weavers who presided over and cut the thread of life and human destinies.

FLOWER

BEAUTY ✳ TRANSIENCE

MEANING OF THE DREAM

Life goes by fast. Enjoy its beauty
without the fear of striving for
the impossible.

MEANING OF THE SYMBOL

A flower is a symbol of transience and beauty. In their funeral rites,
Greeks and Romans adorned themselves with flowers to mark the
reality of death and celebrate the fallen beauty of life. Each color
has its own meaning: yellow refers to radiance, red to blood and
passion, blue to the impossible, white to innocence and sincerity,
and purple to mystery.

FIGURES

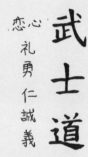

CUBE

MEANING OF THE DREAM

The cube restores an immediate feeling of solidity. It evokes something concluded, an enhancement in one's social and practical life. It is a symbol of equilibrium and the ability to complete plans, alongside a sense of protection and balance.

MEANING OF THE SYMBOL

The cube appears in many allegories of virtue as an emblem of solidity and permanence. For this reason, royal carriages and thrones in symbolic imagery take the form of a cube. As for its concrete connotations, it symbolizes the earth and the physical cosmos, represented in the four elements.

HIEROGLYPH

ENIGMA ✳ ELECTIVE KNOWLEDGE

MEANING OF THE DREAM

The symbolism of the hieroglyph is equivalent to that of the enigma, even if the stylized image is clearly recognizable as an object or animal. It is a sign to interpret, a mystery that only a few, select people can access. It calls for our keen attention.

MEANING OF THE SYMBOL

The hieroglyphic system of Egyptian writing comprised over 900 signs (which could represent ideas, syllables, and words). This made it so complex that only members of the priestly caste were able to decipher it.

TRIANGLE

MEANING OF THE DREAM

A triangle with a higher vertex represents the rising desire for all things. Meanwhile, a triangle with a line through the vertex is the alchemical symbol for air. An inverted triangle symbolizes the heart and may evoke it at when it appears in the dream. The intersection of two triangles creates the six-pointed star or seal of Solomon, which symbolizes the human soul.

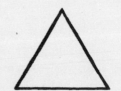

MEANING OF THE SYMBOL

In its broader meaning, the triangle represents the Trinity. A triangle with a pair of horns was the symbol of the Carthaginian goddess Tanit.

NUMBER

MEANING OF THE DREAM

Symbolically, numbers are conceptual pillars. The further they move away from one, the further they sink into worldly material. They archetypically express the harmony of the universe and of ourselves. Even numbers represent passive principles, the odd ones active. Their sequence has great dynamism.

MEANING OF THE SYMBOL

Zero is associated with the non-being of origination, one with the essential emergence of being, two with opposition and conflict, three with spiritual synthesis, four with the earth and the human condition, and five with health and love.

LETTER

SACREDNESS * CORRESPONDENCE

MEANING OF THE DREAM

For the great value attributed to the word, letters have sacred and mystical attributes with a cosmic meaning. They constitute correspondence between language and world, and they open onto a universal order.

MEANING OF THE SYMBOL

Letters have their own symbolic meaning, beyond words. For example, the character "Y" in the Nordic tradition represents the cosmic man with his arms raised, a symbol of resurrection. In the Latin alphabet, "C" represents the waxing moon, the sea, and the Great Mother.

IDEOGRAM

MEANING OF THE DREAM

Despite its apparent indecipherability, the appearance of an ideogram in a dream transmits a symbolic value to us. Ideograms represent the basis of written communication conveying ancient understanding and knowledge.

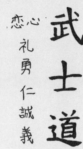

MEANING OF THE SYMBOL

The evolution of Egyptian hieroglyphics and of the three typologies of their script (hieroglyphic, hieratic, demotic) reveals progression from a representative to a conventional form. These symbols evoke the object more than they mention it, while including in it the word's magical power.

COLOR

MEANING OF THE DREAM

Colors correspond to a range of sensations and psychic events. Blue is associated with thought, yellow with knowledge, red with the body and ardent feelings, and green to sensitivity. The spectrum of colors corresponds to their presence in the natural world and the mind's related responses.

MEANING OF THE SYMBOL

The connection between the world's elements through color has been felt since ancient times. The Zuni people of the western United States offer their priests a tribute of the "grans of six colors," each linked to a planetary god.

CRACK

OPENING TO THE IMAGINATION

MEANING OF THE DREAM

A crack indicates that one might be overlooking the world of imagination, a rift in reality that can reveal buried meanings. Dreaming of chapped lips or a house with a crack on the facade reveals that a false person is close to us. If attributed to one's internal self, to time, or to the earth, it represents the abyss into which we fear falling.

MEANING OF THE SYMBOL

In English, "crack" is used not only to indicate a physical crack but also alludes to decoding a secret language, evoking the alchemical power to open the doors of knowledge by filtering light through material.

CIRCLE

TOTALITY * POWER

MEANING OF THE DREAM

There is something that inspires fear in perfection, and perfection is the first psychological meaning of the circle.

MEANING OF THE SYMBOL

First, there were the moon and the sun with their cycles, astral discs considered divine in many cultures. Then came the potter's wheel and the chariot with its wheels, the oldest means of creation and conquest. From ancient times, a complex symbolism began to form associating the circle with a series of meanings linked to the heavens, power, order, fear, and perfection.

ENIGMA

MEANING OF THE DREAM

It is not uncommon for dreams to move through mysterious situations, at times with visions to decipher and others with riddles or paradoxes to unravel. A dream of this type asks us to go deeper into reading into the transcendental, or not immediately visible, facets of an experience.

MEANING OF THE SYMBOL

In many cultures and in various founding myths, the oracle played a fundamental role. Among many peoples, what is presented in the form of an enigma, as unusual or extraordinary, gives rise to miracles and perceivable manifestations of deities, apparitions, and visions.

HUMAN FIGURES

BLACKSMITH

DOMAIN OF PASSIONS * CREATIVITY

MEANING OF THE DREAM

This figure has an ability to direct the red-hot magma of the passions to create lasting, powerful objects. It knows how to direct the inner fire.

MEANING OF THE SYMBOL

The blacksmith is considered someone akin to the cursed poets and unheeded prophets: a creator linked to the astral plane, connected to fire. In some cultures, a blacksmith was the maker of the world with knowledge of how to manipulate the hardness of metals, governing the most powerful and destructive of elements. In others, the craft is a privilege of leaders and is therefore considered sacred.

TWINS

MEANING OF THE DREAM

There is something disturbing about twins: they speak to us of the double, of two things that have an extreme similarity but do not completely match. They remove the safety of the known and imply contrasts: of sky and tree, day and night, heart and soul. They ask that we pay attention to the possible facets of a single event.

MEANING OF THE SYMBOL

Twins exist in most of the world's mythologies; often, they are born from an immortal father and a mortal mother, representing the dual root of human nature. They also symbolize the opposing principles of good and evil.

NEWBORN

TRANSFORMATION ✳ NOVELTY

MEANING OF THE DREAM

The first implication of this symbol is the arrival of a change to do with the inner growth of the dreamer. It could also be linked, however, to the birth of a new project. It is a positive sign, one of hopeful trust in carrying something out.

MEANING OF THE SYMBOL

Innocence, a need for protection, and the future are recurring aspects of the symbolism inherent in an infant's presence. Infants also often serve as an emblem of the radical transformation of given conditions, such as a future king or a savior—a special creature from the moment of its appearance.

MINISTER

MORAL LAW ✳ DUTY

MEANING OF THE DREAM

The appearance of a minister of the divine on earth indicates the existence of or search for a guide. This figure connects us to the spiritual world; it is our conscience speaking to us and reminding us to adhere to the laws of morality, scrupulously fulfilling our duty.

MEANING OF THE SYMBOL

Priests share properties of the sacred, or of separation from parts of the secular world. This is underscored through external signs, such as a shaven head or specific clothing. Mediators between the gods and humans, they are the sole deputies to rites that can keep them in balance.

WARRIOR

ANCESTOR ✴ LATENT FORCE

MEANING OF THE DREAM

A warrior in one's dream indicates the need to rely on the knowledge and power of our ancestors. It symbolizes latent forces in our personality that have readied themselves to assist our conscious mind. If enemy warriors, they represent internal opposing powers that hinder us.

MEANING OF THE SYMBOL

The symbolism of the warrior is similar to that of four archers placed in defense of the cardinal directions in medieval engravings—both defenders and assailants indicating forces that can rebel against synthesis.

LOVER

INTEGRITY * TEMPTATION

MEANING OF THE DREAM

The lover can be read in the same manner as the archetypal symbol existing in tarot card imagery. On a positive note, it expresses making the correct decision, representing integrity and moral beauty. On the other hand, on the negative end, it evokes uncertainty and temptation.

MEANING OF THE SYMBOL

The tarot illustration that depicts an episode in which Hercules must choose between vice and virtue shows a figure who hesitates in choosing between two kinds of conduct. His attire is two-toned, with activity represented in the red half and indecision in the green one.

MOTHER

WISDOM * MERCY

MEANING OF THE DREAM

The figure of a mother in one's dream not only signifies the maternal principle, that of giving impetus to life and caring for it, but more broadly evokes the meaning of a profound, original knowledge that arrives at wisdom. It is also an archetype of unconditional love in an expansive sense, an emblem of mercy.

MEANING OF THE SYMBOL

The mother's representation has been ambivalent in the history of humanity: there is the symbol of the nursing mother and the basis of visceral connection, but also one of the mother that terrifies, a symbol of indifference and death.

WOMAN

SOUL * ACCEPTANCE

MEANING OF THE DREAM

The woman as a young beloved symbolically represents one's own soul. Prior to and beyond her possible transition to mother, she is the wise principle of acceptance of nature (animal, vegetable, and the profound essence of phenomena and people), lunar intuition, and hospitality.

MEANING OF THE SYMBOL

Anthropologically, the female figure has been clad in many attributes—combined with animals, as in the Sphinx or the swan woman in Northern cultures, or gathered into archetypal figures like Sophia or Mary, emblems of science and supreme virtue.

MUSICIAN

FASCINATION WITH DEATH ✳ CONNECTION BETWEEN LIFE AND WILL

MEANING OF THE DREAM

In a dream, a musician playing a sweet melody puts us in touch with the mysterious place uniting life's material world with that which is undifferentiated—that is to say, one's will prior to acting. It expresses the mystery of death that we interrogate deeply and that fascinates us.

MEANING OF THE SYMBOL

According to the ancients, a teenager, almost always a musician, represented a fascination with death. This is refined by the symbolism of the harpist in myth and folklore, as well as the Pied Piper of Hamelin.

DWARF

MEANING OF THE DREAM

A being of small proportions plays an ambivalent role in our dream. This person may be a guardian at the threshold of the unconscious, protecting us from powers outside the sphere of consciousness. If spiteful, however, it reveals the small-mindedness and pettiness of those who are blind to life.

MEANING OF THE SYMBOL

In some myths and in folklore, forest creatures like goblins, gnomes, and dwarves are sometimes protective and helpful toward humans. In other situations, these beings reveal themselves to be of evil character.

GARDENER

GUIDE * ORDER

MEANING OF THE DREAM

The gardener arranges the garden, a place within one's consciousness that is understood to contrast with the forest and free nature of the unconscious. He or she symbolizes a guide who preserves various orientations according to the symbolism of the landscape, guaranteeing form and order.

MEANING OF THE SYMBOL

On the ancestral level, the garden is a female symbol, with the gardener being a custodian of lunar secrets, the figure who from spontaneous fruits of the inner land creates an enclosed, well-kept space.

ANCESTOR

PROTECTION * POSSESSION

MEANING OF THE DREAM

The meaning of an ancestor's appearance in a dream depends on the manner with which they present themselves. They can bring a warning or offer advice, protection, or guidance for everyday life. At the same time, an ancestor may appear threatening or ruthless and can overwhelm, influence, or shame us.

MEANING OF THE SYMBOL

One of the most powerful archetypal incarnations of the ancestors is that of the great goddess Mnemosyne, a deep, ancestral memory, a source of life that becomes an appeal to oneself. Mythically and poetically, she revives the images aroused in the lineage of humanity.

GHOST

MESSAGE * EXHORTATION TO CONCLUDE SOMETHING

MEANING OF THE DREAM

A ghost does not only come in the night to create terror; often, it brings a message or symbolizes unfinished business. It doesn't only bring a request for revenge but also offers protection and advice. In addition to disease, it brings loving gestures and consolation.

MEANING OF THE SYMBOL

There are many traditions all over the world to both tempt and commemorate the spirits of the deceased, including All Saints' Day and Halloween. In China, paper lanterns or boats are placed on the water to indicate the path of the deceased along the course of transmigration.

MUMMY

MEANING OF THE DREAM

A mummy may visit us in order to tell us of a potential psychic rebirth. Visible and invisible elements of change are each immobilized and integrated into a symbol, one universally recognized as a possible form of preservation from death.

MEANING OF THE SYMBOL

Mummification was not practiced only by the Egyptians. Human bodies were also preserved in China and Peru, where the cult of the imperial mummy developed in Incan times.

WITCH

OCCULT * TRUE NATURE

MEANING OF THE DREAM

The witch trades in and regulates the occult, the mysterious powers of the unconscious. She has the ability to lead us to the deepest areas of nature, breaking or creating stasis and movement, instigating and generating decisive transformations. She may represent the magical soil of our rebirth.

MEANING OF THE SYMBOL

In the witch trials held between 1450 and 1700, at least one hundred thousand people died, confirming the fear that any behavior out of the norm could provoke. In folklore especially, from the Russian Baba Yaga to the witches of the Brothers Grimm, this is a figure that nourishes the imagination.

VAMPIRE

MEANING OF THE DREAM

If the vampire that appears in a dream has the appearance of someone known to us, it indicates a harmful power this person has over us, sapping us of our energies. It can also represent a part of us that takes strength from our inner world. It is the manifestation of restlessness, of unprocessed forms of deprivation and traumas.

MEANING OF THE SYMBOL

The history of the vampire has its roots in past centuries, though it was primarily consecrated as a figure of the collective imagination in the Romantic era. An illustrious example is Bram Stoker's novel *Dracula*.

THIEF

VIOLATION ✳ DEPRIVATION

MEANING OF THE DREAM

Internally, theft does not necessarily end in profit: when areas requiring attention do not receive it, it then becomes a psychological form of theft and results in feelings of loss, emptiness, and melancholy. If the person who robs us is known to us, we are warned that he or she is depriving us of something of our internal selves.

MEANING OF THE SYMBOL

There are also sacred thieves in the history of humanity, such as the Scandinavian dwarf Loki, Hermes of Greek mythology, and Krishna of Hindu mythology. Their function is to subvert authority and redistribute gifts.

LIMP

MEANING OF THE DREAM

The presence of someone with
limited mobility conjures a blockage
or a difficulty that prevents the
mobilization of our potential.
The obstacle and disability that
this figure represents in themselves
imply potential for a new vitality
and resources, unknown sources
of dynamism.

MEANING OF THE SYMBOL

In mythology, the deformed foot of blacksmiths and craftsmen symbolizes a magical, virile power drawing its strength from the dark
depths of the psyche. Often it is those who are injured that have
healing powers.

BEGGAR

HUMILITY * FREEDOM

MEANING OF THE DREAM

A beggar presented at the door of our dreams, on the one hand, teaches us of the humility and loyalty of travel companions when adverse conditions bring us to ruin. On the other, it evokes that which we deny ourselves, what impoverishes our lives.

MEANING OF THE SYMBOL

In many myths, there are kings and heroes who hide under a humble guise, to underscore that the highest value can be hidden within simplicity. Both in the East and West, there are sacred beggars who embody freedom, with poverty as a life choice and form of trust in divine compassion.

SEX WORKER

VULNERABILITY * PREDATION

MEANING OF THE DREAM

The nature alluded to by prostitution (male and female) is of a dual nature: there is the negative, of predacious and destructive attitudes, and the positive, of bodily and psychological vulnerability that can inspire solidarity.

MEANING OF THE SYMBOL

The sacred prostitute constitutes a life-giving element embodying a facet of the great divinity of love—be it Aphrodite, Shakti, Ishtar, Inanna, Cybele, or Isis. The great goddess signified a vital power that was mysterious and fertile, with the capacity to cyclically generate, and then regenerate, the universe.

233

KING

MEANING OF THE DREAM

The internal territories that connect with the arrival of a sovereign in our nocturnal world always evoke something regal within us: a lost bond, a desire, a form of seeking. It symbolizes a union of high and low, in which the heroic quest to be undertaken requires sacrifice and adaptability.

MEANING OF THE SYMBOL

With each civilization comes various possible rulers, in that they represent a synthesis of the values considered essential within the psyche, tribe, or society. These are human beings who symbolize the divine stars.

ACROBAT

MEANING OF THE DREAM

You need to position yourself from another perspective and consider things from a new point of view. Do not be afraid of turning what you know up-side down. Welcome the unknown, and it will help you find unprecedented solutions.

MEANING OF THE SYMBOL

Evolutions, fatal leaps, tightrope walking at extraordinary heights – an acrobat is the representation of an upheaval. This figure is a living symbol of the reversal, or a need that presents itself in all one's crises (personal, moral, collective, historical), of creating a break in the current order and overturning it.

ACTIONS AND
HUMAN RELATIONS

FALL

FEAR * LIBERATION

MEANING OF THE DREAM

As in myths and fairy tales, in dreams, we fall from cliffs, buildings, airplanes, and towers. We wish to fly, but our greatest fear is that of plummeting downward, representing a loss of control. Yet falling can also allow for liberation, the escape from a constricting situation.

MEANING OF THE SYMBOL

Mythological heroes run the risk of falling to reach superior knowledge. To extend our horizons and affirm our power over collapse and human limitations, we have always oscillated between feelings of inferiority and conceit. Birth itself is a kind of fall.

DANCING

DYNAMISM * CREATION

MEANING OF THE DREAM

In its rhythm and transformation of the body, dance symbolizes cosmic creation. Every dance is a pantomime of metamorphosis, the dynamic transformation of an existing situation (whether internal or concrete).

MEANING OF THE SYMBOL

The dance of the Hindu deity Shiva symbolizes becoming and embodies eternal energy. The circle of flames that in Hindu iconography surrounds this dancing god relates this cosmogonic function. A dance of intertwined people symbolizes the connection between heaven and earth, cosmic marriage, and union.

BLESSING

GIFT * REQUEST

MEANING OF THE DREAM

Receiving a blessing in a dream, from an authority or a magical or sacred figure, means to receive a gift, a material or spiritual benefit. Meanwhile, asking for a blessing is a form of prayer, a hymn to a person or a situation; it reveals our faith in transcendent forces.

MEANING OF THE SYMBOL

In different times and places, mankind has named the source of all blessings in various ways. Among the best known is mana, a term of Melanesian origin denoting the supernatural qualities of beings or objects, full of power and authority.

NOISE & RHYTHM

EXPRESSION * TEMPTATION

MEANING OF THE DREAM

To make noise and rhythm is to create a celebration (firecrackers exploding, for example) or invocation (as in tribal rites). It signifies a calling of the community's attention and of many internal forces to a specific moment. When these noises are connected to the fervor these can induce, they also evoke the temptation of total abandonment.

MEANING OF THE SYMBOL

Generating noises and percussive rhythms in rituals, ceremonies, and sacred dances is a tradition common throughout the world, in every era. In occidental cultures prior to bells, a percussive instrument was used to call a community gathering.

OATH

LOYALTY * HONOR

MEANING OF THE DREAM

One can perform various actions to take an oath: raise one's hand, touch a sacred object, place a hand on one's chest, or speak a phrase or a word. If one of these signs appears in a dream, we are pledging loyalty to a situation, a person, or a community.

MEANING OF THE SYMBOL

The practice of swearing an oath is found among all peoples and traditions and is a primordial sign of religion. Strictly binding, it can be subject to misuse and abuse, so the sense of honor between the involved parties is very important.

SLEEP

MEANING OF THE DREAM

Sleep is a tangible dividing line during our day, but it is also symbolic in our life. It marks a departure from the ordinary and from what we usually know in waking life.

MEANING OF THE SYMBOL

In various traditions, the symbolisms and rites connected to sleep are linked to the way in which that civilization evaluates death and the themes connected to what seems to be its opposite, namely dawn and awakening. Sleep is a key element of folklore, wherein it can be personified, or where there may be sleeping deities.

PILGRIMAGE

DESTINATION ✳ FRIENDSHIP

MEANING OF THE DREAM

If in a dream we undertake a pilgrimage, we are responding to a powerful destination's call to us. We are also invited to open ourselves to all with whom we will walk the path.

MEANING OF THE SYMBOL

There are many religions that have their places of pilgrimage: Mecca for Muslims; Jerusalem for Muslims, Jews, and Christians; and Ise and Saigoku in Japan, for followers of Shinto and Buddhism respectively. Every pilgrimage presupposes a journey, and a very difficult one, on which the promise of bodily and spiritual healing brings one to forget all adversity.

FLIGHT

ASPIRATION TO RISE ✳ FEAR

MEANING OF THE DREAM

Flight is a symbol of thought and imagination. Often, one dreams of a pleasant sensation moving freely above others and the world. It is our aspiration to rise, a sign of courage and hope. Its opposite, falling, can be the expression of insecurity or the fear of not being able to face something or someone.

MEANING OF THE SYMBOL

In our mythology, the most famous flight is certainly that of Icarus: it axiomatically expresses all the power of self-confidence and superiority—values that, if flaunted, can become risky.

COMBAT

MEANING OF THE DREAM

Combat is the individual aspect of war. To dream of combatting a stranger indicates that a struggle is underway with an unknown, shadowy part of the ego. The impulse to fight is all the stronger the more a person projects their own imperfections onto others.

MEANING OF THE SYMBOL

In past centuries, it was common to challenge someone to a duel, considered a noble method in order to assert one's honor. Challenges were proposed for the most varied reasons, from motives of revenge to issues related to debts not honored, or to matters of theater, literature, or love.

DECAPITATION

REJECTING THE HEAD ✳ SEPARATION

MEANING OF THE DREAM

Cutting the head off from the rest of the body symbolically indicates separation of spiritual aspects of life from the physical and material ones. It also indicates the need for a pause in what or who is guiding us at this moment: a negation of the head, of the guide.

MEANING OF THE SYMBOL

Discovery of the head as the center and seat of spiritual strength dates back to prehistoric times. There are thus many civilizations that have only buried this part of the body or have turned the head into a symbolic ornamental theme.

MARRIAGE

CONCILIATION ∗ COMMUNION

MEANING OF THE DREAM

Marriage represents the intimate union and the internal conciliation between feminine and masculine principles. It is a communion that occurs in the process of identification, in the construction of the complete self that combines unconscious elements with spirit. When another person also appears in the dream, this is a kindred person, an ally in our growth.

MEANING OF THE SYMBOL

In many civilizations, marriage is a founding rite of the community. In alchemy, it actually signifies the Coniunctio, symbolized by the king and queen in the union of sulfur and mercury, the fixed and the volatile.

WORK

MEANING OF THE DREAM

Work symbolizes the constancy and commitment that underlie transformation. Beyond the type of work and the operations it entails, what matters is one's spiritual attitude toward the gift of self that is made by applying oneself with respect to a job or undertaking.

MEANING OF THE SYMBOL

Work holds mystical significance in many traditions. In ancient times, being a farmer was an emblem of patience and dedication. A South Asian legend tells of a cobbler who achieved sainthood thanks to his continual unification of the inferior and the superior.

BITING

MARK * INSTINCT

MEANING OF THE DREAM

The mark of teeth on the body is equivalent to a seal—an imprint of the spirit on the flesh if we also consider teeth to be the walls of the inner human. Dreaming of being bitten by an animal symbolizes the work of instinct upon the psyche.

MEANING OF THE SYMBOL

In some traditions, it is believed that dreaming of a bite heralds an imminent risk. The mythological Greek doctor Asclepius believed that dreaming of a biting snake had healing powers and could aid in discernment.

DEATH

END OF A PERIOD ✳ RENEWAL

MEANING OF THE DREAM

Unlike the negative connotation we apply to death, which frightens us, it has a positive value symbolically. It evokes the conclusion of a period, especially when, resulting from excessive tension, it is presented as a sacrifice.

MEANING OF THE SYMBOL

A popular saying goes that if you dream of someone's death you are extending their life. Death is also the thirteenth Arcanum of the tarot, and as such, it carries a meaning of both ending and of renewal, and of the potential for radical transformation.

NUDITY

PURITY ✳ EXHIBITION

MEANING OF THE DREAM

In dreams, nudity's value differs depending on the sensation with which it is associated. An undressing can be innocent, indicating purity and revealing one's true self. Or it could be sensational, linked to exhibitionist desires. If we attempt to cover ourselves, it reveals insecurity in a situation and distrust in those participating in it.

MEANING OF THE SYMBOL

Among many peoples, the exposure of body parts is not a source of embarrassment but rather has distinctive social functions. Our tradition traces the need to cover oneself back to Adam and Eve, after Original Sin was committed.

BREATH

MEANING OF THE DREAM

The breath is associated with spiritual assimilation. It is closely linked with our emotions: if we dream of ourselves short of breath, we are probably in a situation or state that suffocates and worries us. If, however, we breathe underwater in a dream, it means that we have the capacity to be immersed in our darkest depths.

MEANING OF THE SYMBOL

Breathing plays a central role in yogic practice, as it has the power to calm us and bring us back to the present moment. Our breathing has its own rhythm. When it is fluid and calm, it is in contact with the rhythm of the universe.

SUICIDE

SELF-JUDGMENT ✳ DESIRE FOR TRANSFORMATION

MEANING OF THE DREAM

While in waking life suicide is frightening, in a dream it does not signify a desire to end one's life. Rather, it indicates a moment of severe self-judgment or a desire for profound transformation. It is a moment one wishes to annihilate the old self in order to overcome it.

MEANING OF THE SYMBOL

Suicide is a controversial topic in many civilizations. For the Stoics, it represented a dignified way to deal with misfortunes. Christianity condemns it, while Hindu and Buddhist cultures provide some practices by which it is accepted. In Japanese tradition, there is *harakiri*, a ritual suicide to be committed in the event of failure, injustice, or extreme grief.

MURDER

DIVISION ✳ REVENGE

MEANING OF THE DREAM

On a deep level, killing often has to do with parts of oneself. Even when figures known to us appear in the dream, what we kill is the effect that relationship has within us. Murder also opens up the possibility or a need for revenge; this is related to our primary aggressive drive.

MEANING OF THE SYMBOL

Mythologies and cosmogonies are full of killings, even very bloody ones, which are often perpetrated between family members, very close people, or deities. This demonstrates that violence and abuse are part of human nature.

CRUCIFIXION

PSYCHIC TENSION ✳ ATONEMENT

MEANING OF THE DREAM

The shape of the cross—on which a body is sacrificed in Christian tradition—represents and recalls a psychic tension that can be extreme and heartrending. Its presence in a dream evokes the way in which one is freed from opposites where there is a choice, a voluntary sacrifice of atonement.

MEANING OF THE SYMBOL

The crucifixion of Christ, one of the most powerful extant religious symbols, has affinities with mythological stories, such as Odin's decision to remain hanging from the cosmic tree, pierced by his own blade, in order to obtain wisdom and power.

BURIAL

MEANING OF THE DREAM

Dreaming of burial symbolizes the ability to understand a sign: from ancestral secrets to treasures, to dark sides we have repressed. At the same time, it indicates a waiting phase, one in which the old has disappeared but the new has yet to manifest itself.

MEANING OF THE SYMBOL

Human beings have buried their dead since the Paleolithic age. It is a central moment in the construction of identity and of community. The celebration of the deceased has always served as a social phase to accept mourning and of the human life's transience.

CREMATION

TRANSIENCE * DISPERSION

MEANING OF THE DREAM

Dreaming of cremating someone or being cremated connects us with the symbolic meanings, as well as the physical and psychic mysteries, of fire and ash. It connects us not only to transience but also to the essence and central substance of beings and situations. Being reduced to ashes unites the individual with the whole and eradicates limits.

MEANING OF THE SYMBOL

Ritual cremation, something present in many religions, views fire as a purifying agent that can free the desires, impetuous passions, and bonds of the soul imprisoned within the body of the deceased.

DROWNING

FEELING OVERWHELMED * PREPARATION FOR CHANGE

MEANING OF THE DREAM

Waters that flood our dream until they submerge us indicate a force that overwhelms us: it could be a love affair, an obsession, or a commitment too great for our strength. Yet, through this event, the water that dissolves our previous state is preparing us for a change.

MEANING OF THE SYMBOL

The symbolism of drowning leading to new life is also implicit in Christian baptism and in all founding myths and narratives where a drowned person saves the rest of humanity from floods.

DECOMPOSING

TRANSIENCE ✳ DISPERSION

MEANING OF THE DREAM

Imagery of putrefaction in dreams symbolizes a movement toward the depths of the psyche, a need to get down to the essential, to separate all parts and eliminate those that do not last. It can also be the projection of a moment of creative crisis onto the outside world.

MEANING OF THE SYMBOL

In Canada and Siberia, shamans subjected themselves to terrifying visions in which their sense organs were torn out and left to rot by ferocious spirits. In exchange, they received extraordinary body parts endowed with supernatural powers, such as seers' eyes.

DIGGING

HIDDEN RICHES ✳ DESCENT INTO DARKNESS

MEANING OF THE DREAM

The act of digging in a dream symbolizes the entry to our inner mine, where we can find veins of gold—that is to say, our potential. We can respectfully decide to bring these to light or keep them hidden. They are not to be greedily exploited but protected.

MEANING OF THE SYMBOL

In mythology, elves, Cabiri, and blacksmiths' helpers are often invisible creatures with the ability to transform material. They live deep in the mountains and act as their guardians. They serve the Great Mother and protect her riches.

PLANTING SEEDS

FERTILITY ✳ LACK OF CONTROL

MEANING OF THE DREAM

The act of sowing symbolizes great procreative power, a desire to help something new to grow. As in nature, however, this gesture does not necessarily guarantee success. With this dream, we are then asked to accept what is out of our control.

MEANING OF THE SYMBOL

Sowing is one of the oldest forms of collaboration between man and nature. The word "seminar" also comes from the Latin *semen*, implying a period of study in which ideas are planted in receptive mind.

HUNTING

HEROIC QUEST * DOMINATION

MEANING OF THE DREAM

The hunt can represent the act of going into unknown places to obtain food, in a heroic quest that puts one's life at risk and requires courage. But if hunting is dominated by predation and the pleasure of killing, it implies a desire for domination and possession.

MEANING OF THE SYMBOL

Many myths and fairy tales speak of how the natural and supernatural worlds come together in hunting, archetypically transmitting the risk-filled wonders of defining the individual and of renewal.

SEWING

LANGUAGE ✳ HEROIC HUMILITY

MEANING OF THE DREAM

The act of stitching recalls simple gestures and heroic humility, which through repetition can mend the tears of the soul, a relationship, or an open wound.

MEANING OF THE SYMBOL

The oldest needles, made from sharpened bones, date back to the Paleolithic era, revealing that humans were sewing animal skins together to clothe themselves and keep warm. Weaving is an activity that for many traditions is linked to language; this is indicated in the etymology of "text," from Latin *texere,* or "to interweave."

SHIPWRECK

INVISIBLE DANGER ✳ PRIDE

MEANING OF THE DREAM

Dreaming of a shipwreck puts us face-to-face with potential arrogance, a source of failure. This connects with our fear of oblivion and the reversal of destiny. It involves an awareness of having to face an invisible danger, like reefs hidden by fog on the open sea.

MEANING OF THE SYMBOL

Classical philosophy depicted the body as a ship, on which the captain was the rational soul. The state was represented in the same way, in an iconic image in which citizens collaborated for the common good, to continue on the correct route.

PLAY

INVERSION ✳ LEARNING

MEANING OF THE DREAM

Dreams often bring about images of play; these reveal the subversive aspects of our inner world, which can turn daytime realities upside-down. They illuminate daily processes linked to rivalry, the acceptance of challenges, and the way that we accept defeat and victory.

MEANING OF THE SYMBOL

Many games descend from archaic myths linking the creation of the universe to competition. Chess is based on medieval hierarchies. Games of chance meanwhile descend from divinatory rites. The bell was born as a symbol of the soul's journey through the labyrinth.

INCEST

DESECRATION ✳ RUPTURE

MEANING OF THE DREAM

Incest is one of the most significant taboos in our society, and thus it is disturbing when our unconscious brings it to the surface. The symbolic meaning, however, has to do with uniting with one's own unknown material, breaking or desecrating something prohibited in order to open up a greater awareness.

MEANING OF THE SYMBOL

In myths, incest is often the prerogative of the gods, recalling their archetypal nature and the need for "self-fertilization" in every creative act. In various narratives, it is from incest that the ordered universe or a lineage of divinities is born.

SEXUAL UNION

MEANING OF THE DREAM

Dreaming of sexual intercourse, on the one hand, alludes to the reunion of something that was separate, to a fusion of opposites, to reunification with parts of oneself (perhaps represented by the person being dreamed of). On the other hand, it evokes the unbridled desire for possession, the rituals of supremacy and hostility.

MEANING OF THE SYMBOL

In many Buddhist and Hindu temples, there are models showing pairs of sacred lovers. They are gods caught in the sexual act, staring into each other's eyes, expressing supreme union and the power of love.

KISS

TRANSIENCE * DISPERSION

MEANING OF THE DREAM

In dreams, kisses can have multiple meanings: passion, blessing, recognition, reconciliation, or affection. In a broad sense, they symbolize a trusting openness toward others, exposing and sharing one of the most vulnerable parts of the body. In some cases, an excess of greed can imply the metaphorical need to "eat" the other.

MEANING OF THE SYMBOL

In different cultures, kissing is not just an act of love, bliss, or humility. It can also allude to betrayal and double-dealing: think of the role of Judas.

SWIMMING

FANTASY ✳ SALVATION

MEANING OF THE DREAM

The sensation of swimming in a dream is like that of flying: the ability to move freely and to perform playful gestures that are not possible on land, in conscious life. The act of swimming represents the freedom of the imagination but also, if we run the risk of drowning, the only recourse to safety.

MEANING OF THE SYMBOL

Swimming can be seen as practicing a fusion with nature, a regenerating immersion in sacred waters, or a return to the origin (the mother's womb, the beginning of our species' development).

DRINKING

MEANING OF THE DREAM

You are ready to quench your soul with something that can transform you. Don't be afraid to drink from the cup that fate offers you.

MEANING OF THE SYMBOL

Drinking or offering to drink, as a gesture, is part of many religious and magical rituals. From magical elixirs and shamanic potions to the wine of Christian communion, consecrated during mass, the act of drinking symbolizes the assimilation of virtue, doctrines, knowledge, life, and change.

ELEMENTS AND SYMBOLIC FIGURES

VORTEX

TRANSITION * REVELATION

MEANING OF THE DREAM

A vortex pulls you to mysterious places that can signify both dangerous perdition and great calm all at once. The effect of the psyche's forces can be equally dual in nature, pushing us from terror to hope through a motivation to change.

MEANING OF THE SYMBOL

In many legends, positive aspects of the vortex combine with its violent ones: we are pushed into a chaos that becomes an initiation. The center of this danger brings forth a vision that is usually hidden. It is a portal to other worlds and times, and it allows us a glimpse into the realm of the dead.

FLOOD

DEVASTATION * FORESIGHT

MEANING OF THE DREAM

Periods of great change, forays into the unconscious, loss of contact. The tides of our inner world can overwhelm us in unpredictable ways. We can survive these by heeding warnings that come from unusual sources, such as dreams and visions.

MEANING OF THE SYMBOL

Many origin stories tell of small groups of animals or families that survive a flood, as if to remind us that the first step toward rebirth begins with nourishing a small bit of matter. Providence, luck, and guile are allies in promoting the recovery that comes with each flood.

BUBBLE

INFINITY * SPIRITUAL PERFECTION

MEANING OF THE DREAM

The archetypal bubble is described by mystics as "the perfect nothingness, source of everything." Its roundness represents unity, yet its fragility reminds us of the unreliability and instability of everything, despite its symbolizing eternal life. It can also signify flying in dreams.

MEANING OF THE SYMBOL

The translucent bubble, with its reflection of the rainbow and perfectly round shape, has inspired the contemplation of the infinite and the eternal over the centuries. Unity and wholeness combine with its semi-transparency, a symbol of the numinous and of spirituality.

TOTEM

BELONGING ✳ ORIGIN

MEANING OF THE DREAM

A totem is an emblem that shows belonging to a community and recognizing oneself in a group. It is a sacred element of connection with the ancestors, to whom offerings are brought. It guides us, protects us, and, if animal, lends us its characteristics.

MEANING OF THE SYMBOL

It is thought that totemism was the basis of ancient Egyptian religion and may be somehow connected with the Greco-Roman pantheon. Today, it still persists in indirect forms, in its representation of a group's identity and mythical origin (think of team names or collectives).

ELIXIR

YOUTH * UNDERTAKING

MEANING OF THE DREAM

The elixir, or magical drink, is a substance linked to the idea of eternal youth and the capacity to cure all evils and cause what appears withered to flourish again. It likewise evokes the feat necessary to acquire it, implicit in every "hero's journey."

MEANING OF THE SYMBOL

In Egyptian, Hindu, Greek, Babylonian, and Jewish myths, life emerges from the waters, denoting the existence of a water of life that can generate and regenerate. In tribal traditions, elixirs are available to the community.

278

GATE

PATH ✳ TRANSITION

MEANING OF THE DREAM

A gate serves as both a path and a magical place where inside and outside come together. It provides access to another world, a space that is both an end and a beginning. It could take the form of an entrance to a cave or a pile of stones, though this transition point's most familiar expression is that of the threshold.

MEANING OF THE SYMBOL

The gate is used as a symbol in civic monuments. Among these, famous examples include the entry gate at the Taj Mahal in India, the entrance that leads to the temple of the sleeping Buddha in China, and Ghiberti's *Gates of Paradise* in Florence.

DEVIL

MEANING OF THE DREAM

The devil can appear in various forms within a dream, often taking the shape of a potential temptation. The classic form coming from the Christian imagination with horns, trident, and goat legs might be explicit or referential in its detail. The unconscious speaks to us of a stagnation or regression and of reliance on instinct.

MEANING OF THE SYMBOL

As the fifteenth Arcanum of the tarot, the devil denotes the four elements in tension with one another. He is linked to desire in all its possible forms, with the disorder and strength of the passions.

HOLE

OTHERWORLDLY ACCESS ✳ FERTILITY

MEANING OF THE DREAM

A hole is a symbol of great importance, connected to the potential to inseminate our consciousness and existence, opening them to other possible worlds. In this manner, it connects to the wound, a tear of sorts favoring passage from one reality to another.

MEANING OF THE SYMBOL

Many "hollow" stones are objects of worship throughout the world. One of these rocks still exists in a part of France, for example, where women go to pray for the health of their children. The hole is a door that allows for the soul's journey.

MERMAID

TEMPTATION ✳ DANGER

MEANING OF THE DREAM

When a mermaid's siren song bewitches our sleep, it signifies the presence of a very strong temptation, a spell that we can only escape with enormous effort. It also warns us that this craving carries very high risks, capable of casting us overboard and leading us to self-destruction.

MEANING OF THE SYMBOL

In many traditions, mermaids are terrible monsters with the capacity to drive human beings to death or madness. Only in the fairy tales of modern times have they transformed into the beautiful, benign creatures that little ones enjoy so much.

ANGEL

MESSENGER * HARBINGER OF POSSIBILITIES

MEANING OF THE DREAM

An angel can manifest itself in
a dream in a celestial choir, in
animal or human form, gendered
or androgynous, and as a cloud, a
star, or fire. As the term's etymology
makes clear, it signifies the arrival of
a messenger, and it suggests omens
of new possibilities that we are
consciously not yet able to conceive.

MEANING OF THE SYMBOL

In addition to Christian sacred depictions, angel-like figures appear
in many other cultures; think of the Hindu and Buddhist apsaras, the
Tibetan dakinis, or the ba of Egyptian mythology.

UNICORN

CREATIVE POWER ✳ PURITY

MEANING OF THE DREAM

The unicorn, an emblem of our most creative and hidden unconscious, instructs us to follow the most dynamic and powerful energies channeled through the invisible world, synthesized in the magical powers of its horn. Its appearance also implies faith in the purity of our inspiration.

MEANING OF THE SYMBOL

The Chinese unicorn had animal features and lived in the forest, with a voice akin to the tinkling of monastery bells. His glimmering body was a symbol of benevolence, wisdom, and longevity.

MONSTER

INFERIOR POWERS ✳ EXCESS

MEANING OF THE DREAM

The monster frightens us because it represents the emergence of insidious powers that can put us in danger: excess imagination, impure intentions, the darkest and deepest layers.
A fight with the monster symbolizes the struggle to free the conscious mind bridled by the unconscious.

MEANING OF THE SYMBOL

The depiction of monsters has been constant through the history of art from Neolithic to historical cultures. It decreases in the Gothic period, when images of salvation prevail and monsters constitute an expression of fear, then is resumed by Romanticism and dominated by fantastical creatures.

OGRE

TIME ✳ FOREWARNING

MEANING OF THE DREAM

The ogre often appears in human form, although gigantic in size. The threat of his devouring a child, that is, our inner child, signifies the passage of time for every creature. It is a warning and a sign to be more mindful of one's time.

MEANING OF THE SYMBOL

The figure of the ogre in popular fairy tales originates from Saturn, the god who devoured his children as Cybele brought them into the world. He is the "terrible father" one must come to terms with, serving a cathartic function.

CYCLOPS

WILD FORCES * ROUGHNESS

MEANING OF THE DREAM

When a being with only one eye appears, it speaks to a lack of spiritual subtlety and the coarseness of those who cannot see deeply at the given moment. If it is a giant but not a Cyclops, it is the force of the wild come alive, acting without heeding one's mind and conscience.

MEANING OF THE SYMBOL

The most well-known Cyclops is Polyphemus, as recounted by Homer. The Cyclops were described by Hesiod as the children of Gaea and Uranus. Responsible for metalwork and the manufacture of lightning, they were associated with thunder, lightning bolts, and brightness.

KNOT

CONNECTION * BINDING

MEANING OF THE DREAM

Tying a knot in a dream evokes the tightening of a given situation or relationship into an enclosed connection. This may also be an indication of something too narrow or that imprisons or bridles. To untie the knot is to find the essence at the center.

MEANING OF THE SYMBOL

The knot has symbolically been invested with magical powers, corresponding to the idea of being able to maintain "ties" from afar. The gesture is therefore connected to concepts of curses, slander, and travel. The myth of the Gordian knot, cut by Alexander the Great, symbolizes the resolution of a seemingly insurmountable problem via extreme measures.

GRAIL

INTEGRATION * ONE'S OWN ESSENCE

MEANING OF THE DREAM

Although the grail is generally depicted as a cup, it can take on many forms; these correspond to the inner life of those who set out in search of it. It symbolizes a desire to reach the essence of one's expressiveness as well as one's potential, completeness, integration, and fulfillment.

MEANING OF THE SYMBOL

In Nordic traditions, the grail is associated with a cauldron of abundance and knowledge. In Christian times, it became the mythical cup wherein drops of the crucified Christ's blood were collected.

FURIES

MEANING OF THE DREAM

The Furies can appear in multiple forms, representing vindictive and merciless ire against the betrayal of primary values. If repressed, they risk a brutal explosion, bringing us humiliation. If we allow them to act deeply, however, they can bring repair.

MEANING OF THE SYMBOL

Rage, revenge, madness, and remorse form the basis of the Furies' archetype, portrayed in many myths in the act of avenging the basest crimes, such as those perpetrated against family members.

SHADOW

DOUBLE ✳ DARK SIDE

MEANING OF THE DREAM

The shadow that appears in a dream symbolizes our double—what we consider inferior and unvirtuous that we always carry with us. It is also our dark side, a container of impulses, thoughts, and emotions that we tend to reject or dismiss.

MEANING OF THE SYMBOL

In many cultures, the shadow has a similar meaning to the double, to the concept of the mirror and to a reflection on water. It represents the soul, a vital element of oneself, and for this reason it is feared that it will be stolen or injured. Should this happen, the consequences of this loss on a person would be devastating.

FAIRIES

SUPERNATURAL POWERS OF THE SOUL * HONEST ABILITIES

MEANING OF THE DREAM

It is time for your hidden faculties to come to light. Unexpected resources, that you almost did not believe you had, are now able to be manifested.

MEANING OF THE SYMBOL

In the esoteric view, fairies symbolize the supernatural powers of the human soul. They also represent people's hidden potential. Fairies themselves actually disguise their extraordinary powers and great wisdom, exercising common or humble trades (the Fates, for example, are spinners).

WOUND

TRAUMA * OPENING

MEANING OF THE DREAM

A wound is a break in one's physical or psychic fabric, a trauma that leads to a change and the revelation of hidden energies or needs. The wound is something to which one tends, the medium through which profound energies emerge. To ignore these threatens the integrity of the whole.

MEANING OF THE SYMBOL

When Jacob fought against the angel of God, he was wounded in the thigh, symbolizing the encounter with and shocking openness to the divine. It is the traumatic breach wherein a new mode of relating to ourselves and others congeals.

PLACES

OCEAN

DEPTH ✳ WISDOM

MEANING OF THE DREAM

The vastness of the ocean parallels the depths of our mind and our memory. In both, the deepest regions are inaccessible. We can nourish our knowledge through the emotional tempests, fathoming the depths of our conscience, transported by a wave of creative inspiration.

MEANING OF THE SYMBOL

Ancient and primordial, the ocean is the original creator of life and an expression of adventure, danger, and travel. Yet those who traverse and explore it return rich in wisdom, aware of archetypal epicenters of powerful and upsetting energies.

CAVE

MEANING OF THE DREAM

Dreaming of entering a cave represents the potential to find a safe refuge from something we feel threatens us. This cave symbolizes the womb of Mother Earth. It can also, however, signify a restricted and archaic perspective or an overwhelming insecurity.

MEANING OF THE SYMBOL

Caves and caverns formed humans' first homes, and for this reason as well, they have always been rich in symbolic importance. One famous interpretation is Plato's, describing life itself as a cave for those who ignore the light of truth.

CITY

EVOLUTION ✱ ONE'S OWN CENTER

MEANING OF THE DREAM

A city, be it a small center or a metropolis, symbolizes our conscious ventures, our progress, and how the steps we take evolve; under its visible foundations lie those of the previous civilization, or our old way of being. It is our center, the place exchanges, initiatives, and relationships take place.

MEANING OF THE SYMBOL

Cities, especially ancient ones, are built upon the principles of sacred geometry, including circles, squares, diamonds, and crosses, where the main roads extend in the cardinal directions.

CASTLE

DEFENSE ✳ CONSTRAINT

MEANING OF THE DREAM

The castle is an emblem of the ability
to create safety, enclosing our dearest
and most revealing within a fortress.
This shelter is reinforced, turreted,
walled, and closed by a drawbridge,
safeguarding everything inside.
However, if we are not able to exit, it
becomes a constraint, a lack of free
choice.

MEANING OF THE SYMBOL

The castle represents the place of power, where the rulers and the
treasures are guarded. Saint Teresa of Ávila compared the soul to a
crystal castle with many chambers, with God and soul uniting at its
center.

WELL

ACCESS TO MYSTERY * UNDERGROUND NOURISHMENT

MEANING OF THE DREAM

To dream of a well evokes the opening of a door accessing the mystery of our soul. Symbolically, it is an invitation directed toward one's conscience to care for and pay attention to the deep flows surging in our depths in order to be nourished by them.

MEANING OF THE SYMBOL

There are numerous sacred wells in many cultures. As a source of water to the community, the well is a central, precious place, to such a degree that it is considered the home of divinities and spirits, as well as a source of prophecies, miracles, and the ability to realize desires.

TEMPLE

MEANING OF THE DREAM

A temple represents a sacred space full of deep energy where our center shines forth. It is the place around which our world revolves and that defines our place in the general order of things.

MEANING OF THE SYMBOL

In addition to religious, linguistic, cultural, and temporal distinctions, the temple, understood as a place separate from lay life, is a call to enter spirituality. Some Eastern sanctuaries have domes summoning the protection of the celestial vault, while many other temples call upon forms of sacred geometry.

CLOISTER

CULTIVATING ONE'S OWN FRUITS * IMPRISONMENT

MEANING OF THE DREAM

The cloister, where a monk takes care of his protected garden, is a symbol of the necessary solitude in which we may cultivate our fruits. But the root of the term is the same as that of "claustrophobia," the feeling of being imprisoned, which we also experience when we suffocate the life we truly desire.

MEANING OF THE SYMBOL

The cloister, in its closed, protected form, reflects the act of a meditative walk around one's inner core, for the sake of expanding it. In the Middle Ages, this was where one's potential was allowed to flourish.

TOWER

HIERARCHY ✶ FEMALE POWER

MEANING OF THE DREAM

A tower standing vertically creates a clear hierarchy between high and low, between those who have power and those who do not. As a place for keeping princesses and maidens, who represent the soul and female power, the challenges they face in escaping it indicate the strength it takes to free these energies.

MEANING OF THE SYMBOL

Ziggurats, pyramids, and Mayan architecture constitute constructions that evoke the image of the cosmic mountain. They rise as an expression of the human need to reach the heavens, a need that can lead to arrogance and thus be punished by the gods.

TUNNEL

ESCAPE * MAKING HEADWAY

MEANING OF THE DREAM

If in our dream we find ourselves in a tunnel or we are digging one, we are symbolically attempting to find a way inside of ourselves or to find our way out of imposed conventions. A tunnel can also be an emblem of escape from a situation into which we feel forced.

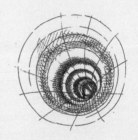

MEANING OF THE SYMBOL

Some initiation and healing rites had initiands pass through a tunnel made of animal skins as a symbol of rebirth and healing. In part, it serves as a refuge, but most especially a place of transition.

ROAD

PASSAGE ✳ SEPARATION

MEANING OF THE DREAM

If we dream of the street where we lived during childhood, we are highlighting a sense of security and, at the same time, of limitation. A street indicates a dutiful involvement, a crossing, and a continuing onward to transform our lives. It can also signify separation, if what we wish to reach lies on the other side of the street.

MEANING OF THE SYMBOL

The way a road is characterized has varied significantly from one era to another, evolving in parallel with civilization. This depends on its placement within a city, as well as the people and the businesses occupying it.

SCHOOL

DEVELOPMENT ✴ UNSOLVED CONFLICT

MEANING OF THE DREAM

To dream of being back at school, perhaps anxious about a task or an exam, reflects a moment of arrest in the personality's development, anxieties that are now ready to be unlocked. It may also indicate old unresolved conflicts that manifest themselves in new ways.

MEANING OF THE SYMBOL

The Greek and Latin roots of the word "school" were connected to leisure time or, better, idleness—that special moment dedicated to growth, dialogue, debate, and lessons

PRISON

MEANING OF THE DREAM

Symbolically, the prison represents a constraining bond to which our ego is subjected—detaining not only physically but through humiliation, ridicule, or degradation. It also evokes a punishment for offenses against the integrity of the self. Ultimately, it is an emblem of the responsibilities we attempt to evade.

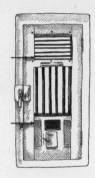

MEANING OF THE SYMBOL

Gnosticism claimed that matter held back and bridled the virtuous part of the world, and that the body itself was a prison for the soul.

DESERT

DISORIENTATION ✳ NEW EXPERIENCE

MEANING OF THE DREAM

If we dream that we are in a desert area, it signifies a moment of disorientation, tedium, and thirst for creativity. But the desert is a place not only of deprivations but also of new experiences and revelations: angels, demons, or genies appear. We are thus able to find new sources of inspiration.

MEANING OF THE SYMBOL

The desert is a metaphor for resilience and adaptability, like those of nomadic peoples surviving in the desolate areas of the Arabian Peninsula, Africa, China, America, Russia, and the South Pole.

UNDERWORLD

IMMERSION ✳ TRANSFORMATIVE POWER

MEANING OF THE DREAM

To dream of descending into the underworld is a metaphor for a need to fully experience everyday life, to immerse oneself in the liveliest fire of passions, responsibilities, failures, and psyche to be able to ascend into a new life. Navigating the underworld has a great transformative power.

MEANING OF THE SYMBOL

The descent to the underworld reinterprets Egyptian mythology, in which the sun takes a "nighttime journey" by sea to the underworld before returning to a new day. It appears in mythology as Aeneas's and Orpheus's journeys to the underworld, and in religion as Christ's descent into Limbo.

WORLD

ORDER * PARADISE FOUND

MEANING OF THE DREAM

The world can appear to us in a dream as an image of our planet seen from space, but also as a geographical map or a sensation. It speaks of planetary order, finding or looking for one's own place. It can also be understood to be a place that has been lost, a paradise found.

MEANING OF THE SYMBOL

All great symbols are images of the world, from the seven-armed candelabra to the mandala, to the zodiac, to tarot cards. The conjunction of opposites that these represent is evoked through imagery marrying the square and the circle in a simple fashion.

MOUNTAIN

PURPOSE ✳ ELEVATION

MEANING OF THE DREAM

The climbing of a mountain directly accounts for effort, sacrifice, and the possibility of falling. At the same time, it clarifies our purpose in proceeding and identifies the scope of such courage. Finally, those who take on the challenge are taken to a place where earth and sky come to meet.

MEANING OF THE SYMBOL

Many peoples have sacred mountains, considered a source of life from which everything descends, protectors, and places where venerable creatures live. One of the best known is Mount Fuji, a symbol of Japan, a safeguard of temples and the destination of multiple pilgrimages.

VALLEY

MEANING OF THE DREAM

The valley, when desolate or dark, represents a low point in life, an area of depression or stagnation. When traversed, it constitutes a concrete experience, in contrast to the transcendent one of mountains. If rich and luxuriant, with water and vegetation, it indicates possibility and refreshment after a long period of hard work.

MEANING OF THE SYMBOL

Emblematic of the valley's significance is the Egyptian Valley of the Kings, where pharaohs were buried. Surrounded by steep rock faces, it remains a place of peace, rest, immortality, and silent reflection.

MARSH

MEANING OF THE DREAM

Moving through or being stuck in a swamp could be interpreted as a sign of immobility and bondage, while in reality, it symbolizes a merely temporary yet necessary transition within a larger process. It is an unpredictable, slippery, vulnerable phase, and as such vital and still evolving—to be handled with care.

MEANING OF THE SYMBOL

In ancient civilizations, the marsh symbolized energies of dissolution that came from the founding waters of life, the emblem of a cycle containing danger but also renewal.

ISLAND

UNFORESEEN SPACE ✳ SELF-CENTEREDNESS

MEANING OF THE DREAM

The island symbolizes a temporary space of solitude and peace, an unexpected place in which to stop, where one can look for treasures. If it conveys a sense of claustrophobia, it can indicate a self-centered outlook or moment coming from restricted, narcissistic, or inaccessible views.

MEANING OF THE SYMBOL

In mythologies throughout the world, islands often constitute places where oracles or dangerous, seductive creatures live, places of refuge and bliss, or mysterious kingdoms of the dead. They are places to live out unexpected adventures.

CROSSROADS

MEANING OF THE DREAM

Even in everyday language, being at a crossroads expresses a place of indecision, a potential turning point. In a dream, it confirms that, even if there seems to be no way out of the situation in which we find ourselves, we always have a choice. It also reminds us of the commitment we have toward our own path.

MEANING OF THE SYMBOL

Legends show that when pacts are made with the devil, it happens at an intersection. It is a place bridging the material and immaterial, where mortals can attune themselves with the invisible world.

LABYRINTH

CONFUSION ✳ CLARITY

MEANING OF THE DREAM

If we dream of a labyrinth, it means that we are in a state of confusion and having difficulty unraveling a situation. It is a distressing and illogical place yet contains the answers within itself: one must simply pick oneself up to find the solution and the way out. It contains the clarity of the path we must take if we look at things from another perspective.

MEANING OF THE SYMBOL

In some initiatory rites, a labyrinth is used to create a temporary feeling of loss, in order to remove someone's sense of orientation via rational coordinates and create access to another form of knowledge.

CELLAR

FOUNDATION * NEED TO GO IN-DEPTH

MEANING OF THE DREAM

To dream of hearing suspicious sounds in the basement can indicate a need for in-depth analysis, to understand whether what is to come should be accommodated or stopped. It symbolizes the foundations upon which we build any of our psychic, evolutionary, or emotional constructions.

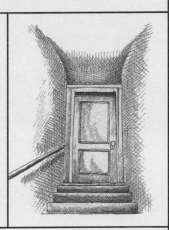

MEANING OF THE SYMBOL

An underground chamber is not only a place where one keeps stock for the winter but also a violent symbol of all that is repressed and linked to the realm of the dead. Underground chambers can be prisons, places connected to matter and our most earthly, material elements.

ATTIC

SEDIMENT * CONCRETE EXPERIENCE

MEANING OF THE DREAM

In order to reach the attic, one must climb to the uppermost floor, which represents the head. Its low ceiling, however, requires a bending over the concrete experience of our past life. There are personal and family issues lying beneath the surface, asking for order and understanding of what must be kept and what should be let go.

MEANING OF THE SYMBOL

The attic is the environment treated, especially in literature, as a place where fugitives can be hidden, murders are carried out, humble families can live, and unwelcome people are locked up.

WALL

MEANING OF THE DREAM

When an image of a wall, or of any obstacle that prevents us from proceeding, appears, it symbolizes a sense of inability to continue along a path taken. It constitutes a momentary difficulty or something inaccessible, whether experiential or spiritual.

MEANING OF THE SYMBOL

Depending on the respective context, anything surrounded by barriers, such as a garden surrounded by high walls or a fortified city, represents an earthly or spiritual reality to which you desire access. Ingenuity and courage will be required to attain it.

EGYPT

MEANING OF THE DREAM

Egypt may appear in a dream as a symbol of a spiritual need. It calls back to the Valley of the Kings, an immortal place beyond time, full of the mystery and fascination of thousands of years. If one sees the pyramids, where hidden treasures and pharaoh sarcophagi can be found, it indicates the allure of the unexplored.

MEANING OF THE SYMBOL

Many of the rituals, mythologies, and sacred stories that came from ancient Egypt have had an influence, direct and indirect, on our civilizations—the cult of the sun, first and foremost.

PARTY

MEANING OF THE DREAM

If we find ourselves at a party in a dream, we are bringing to mind the importance of celebrating a person or an event (either internal or external). We are placing emphasis on something or someone, and we feel that this can best be done if it happens collectively, implying a need to share.

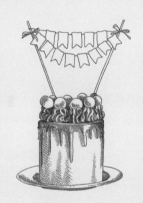

MEANING OF THE SYMBOL

Modern holidays are a transposition of ancient rites, which took place on a regular basis, generally every year. For the Celts, for example, the most important of these fell on November 1, when inaccessible forces mingled with humans.

SUBWAY

CONQUEST ✳ DISRUPTION

MEANING OF THE DREAM

The bustle of the subway calls to mind an expansion of consciousness in multiple directions. It collects all the action of the city above and transforms it into a conquest of new spaces, symbolizing, in part, a shocking change. It maintains, however, the disturbances and fears related to underground worlds.

MEANING OF THE SYMBOL

The subway contains in itself all the charm expressed in the myths of the subsoil, as a dark kingdom in which possible and impossible touch each other. It also brings about a phobia of closed places and getting lost in the crowd.

AIRPLANE

MEANING OF THE DREAM

The nightmares and apocalypses of medieval times have today been replaced by fears of airline crashes and bombings, a reminder of how mechanical flight is essentially perceived as a transgression from the norm, a form of human overconfidence. Boarding a plane also symbolizes the possibility of escape and reaching lofty, distant goals.

MEANING OF THE SYMBOL

The desire to fly traces back to the flight of shamans and of angels, the myth of Icarus, and the levitation of yogi. It affirms the potential of human ingenuity.

TRAIN

MEANING OF THE DREAM

Being on a train, or feeding a coal engine, symbolizes the possibility to channel great energy to be able to reach one's destination or goal. It can also represent a fear of being late or of irreparably losing an opportunity.

MEANING OF THE SYMBOL

The train has often been associated with fate or death, evoking the passage of life with its traversal of various landscapes. It is a place where one can eat and sleep while moving, bringing together the allure of the present and of eternity.

CAR

GOAL ✳ SUCCESS

MEANING OF THE DREAM

The way we dream of a car speaks to our attitude toward our use of time and way of life: if we are behind the wheel, stuck in traffic, if we fear a malfunction, or if we have difficulty operating the brakes. If someone else is driving, it indicates that we are being dragged along by a force or a person.

MEANING OF THE SYMBOL

The car symbolizes a milestone reached, since a license to drive comes when one reaches a certain age of maturity. The type of car also represents some of our external features, as an emblem of success and a status symbol.

SWIMMING POOL

CONTAINMENT OF ENERGY * PSYCHIC LIFE

MEANING OF THE DREAM

In a dream, the modern rectangular swimming pool, a work of human labor, represents the ability to contain energy, something also underscored by the exercises that can be done there. The swimming pool is a container of the aqueous sources of our psychic life, which must be continually renewed to prevent a stagnant pool from forming.

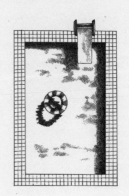

MEANING OF THE SYMBOL

In ancient Egyptian frescos, the garden pond represents both a domesticated form of nature and a small portion of the infinite, brought into the midst of daily life.

FOUNTAIN

EXCHANGE ✳ INSPIRATION

MEANING OF THE DREAM

Taking water from a fountain, drinking, and being refreshed are symbols of access to eternal youth, a drawing of new lifeblood vivifying our sense of inspiration. The fountain is a place of exchange, where the water of its source is channeled for use in an unending yet disciplined flow.

MEANING OF THE SYMBOL

The fountain is a universal image of living waters that vivify spirit and body. It is at the center of the garden of Venus, it symbolizes Mercury, who regulates transformation, and it embodies the female principle of an abundant source.

GARDEN

INNER SECRET CONSCIOUSNESS

MEANING OF THE DREAM

You must withdraw into yourself and cultivate your inner world. Consciousness calls to you, and only you know the secret, the pact, the treasure that you keep.

MEANING OF THE SYMBOL

The garden is the place where nature is put to order and bent to the will of reason. It therefore symbolizes consciousness, in contrast with the wild forest, which represents the unconscious. Yet the garden is also the perfect hiding place for keeping treasures and secrets, or a sweet shelter where pacts of love are made.

WOODS

SOMETHING PRIMORDIAL * WILD

MEANING OF THE DREAM

The tangle of the forest, where we lose our orientation, symbolizes what is on the edge of the typical civil, conscious world. It represents the primordial that survives in us, inhabited by wild animals and magical creatures who can guide us or alert us to danger.

MEANING OF THE SYMBOL

Devotees to Shiva went to the ancient sacred woods to heal their evils and be in communion. Stories from folklore are full of forests, places a hero must go to face and overcome his fears.

INDEX

AZZURRA D'AGOSTINO

Author, scholar of anthropology, and enthusiast of fortune-telling and tarot, Azzurra D'Agostino was born and lives in a small town in the Tuscan-Emilian Apennines. She has published collections of poetry, for which she has received several prizes. She writes for the theater, both for adult audiences and for children. She has published books for children and young adult novels. She is the author of the *Oracle of Destiny* deck.

FEDERICA DE FAZIO

Illustrator and expert in engraving techniques, Federica de Fazio lives in Puglia, where she works as an illustrator. She collaborates with numerous publishing houses, Italian and international, on independent and personal projects.

Publisher
Balthazar Pagani

Graphic design
Bebung

Vivida

Vivida® is a registered trademark property of White Star s.r.l.
www.vividabooks.com

© 2024 White Star s.r.l.
Piazzale Luigi Cadorna, 6
20123 Milano, Italia
www.whitestar.it

Translation: Megan Bredeson
Editing: Abby Young

Rights to the total or partial translation,
reproduction, and adaptation by any means
are reserved for all countries.

ISBN 978-88-544-2086-1
1 2 3 4 5 6 28 27 26 25 24

Printed in China